C000242736

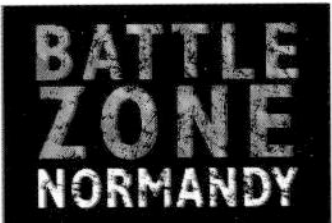

BATTLE FOR CAEN

The 'Battle Zone Normandy' Series

Orne Bridgehead Lloyd Clark
Sword Beach Ken Ford
Juno Beach Ken Ford
Gold Beach Simon Trew
Omaha Beach Stephen Badsey & Tim Bean
Utah Beach Stephen Badsey
Villers-Bocage George Forty
Battle for Cherbourg R.P.W. Havers
Operation Epsom Lloyd Clark
Battle for St-Lô Peter Yates
Battle for Caen Simon Trew & Stephen Badsey
Operation Cobra Christopher Pugsley
Road to Falaise Stephen Hart
Falaise Pocket Paul Latawski

All of these titles can be ordered via the Sutton Publishing website www.suttonpublishing.co.uk

The 'Battle Zone Normandy' Editorial and Design Team

Series Editor Simon Trew
Senior Commissioning Editor Jonathan Falconer
Assistant Editor Nick Reynolds
Cover and Page Design Martin Latham
Editing and Layout Donald Sommerville
Mapping Map Creation Ltd
Photograph Scanning and Mapping Bow Watkinson
Index Chantal Hamill

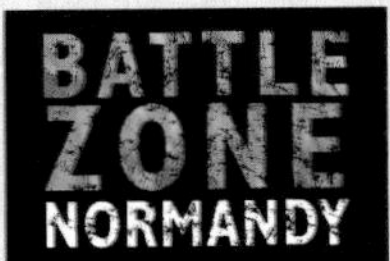

BATTLE FOR CAEN

SIMON TREW
&
STEPHEN BADSEY

Series Editor: Simon Trew

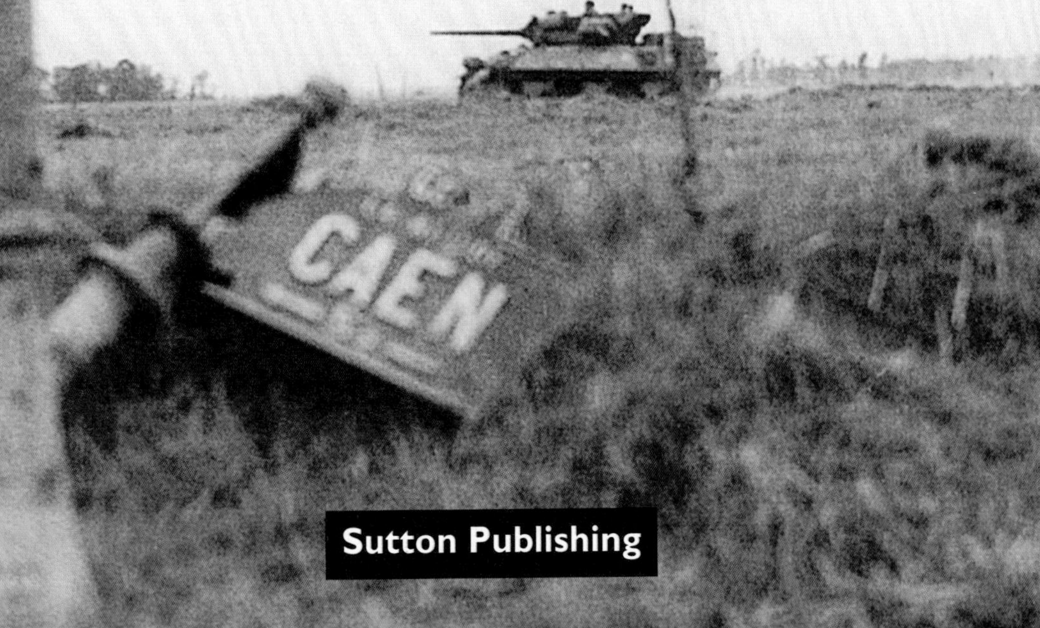

Sutton Publishing

First Published in 2004 by
Sutton Publishing Limited · Phoenix Mill
Thrupp · Stroud · Gloucestershire · GL5 2BU

Text Copyright © Stephen Badsey & Simon Trew 2004
Tour map overlays Copyright © Sutton Publishing
Tour base maps Copyright © Institut Géographique National, Paris
GSGS (1944) map overlays Copyright © Sutton Publishing
GSGS (1944) base maps Copyright © The British Library/Crown Copyright

All rights reserved. No part of this publication may be reproduced, stored in a retrieval system, or transmitted, in any form or by any means, electronic, mechanical, photocopying, recording or otherwise, without the prior permission of the publisher and copyright holder.

Stephen Badsey & Simon Trew have asserted the moral right to be identified as the authors of this work.

British Library Cataloguing in Publication Data
A catalogue record for this book is available from The British Library.

ISBN 0-7509-3010-1

While every effort has been made to ensure that the information given in this book is accurate, the publishers, the authors and the series editor do not accept responsibility for any errors or omissions or for any changes in the details given in this guide or for the consequence of any reliance on the information provided. The publishers would be grateful if readers would advise them of any inaccuracies they may encounter so these can be considered for future editions of this book. The inclusion of any place to stay, place to eat, tourist attraction or other establishment in this book does not imply an endorsement or recommendation by the publisher, the series editor or the authors. Their details are included for information only. Directions are for guidance only and should be used in conjunction with other sources of information.

Typeset in 10.5/14 pt Sabon

Printed and bound in England by
J.H. Haynes & Co. Ltd, Sparkford

Front cover: A Canadian Sherman tank advances into Caen, 10 July 1944. *(National Archives of Canada [NAC] PA-162667)*

Page 1: Monument to 59th (Staffordshire) Division in Galmanche. *(Simon Trew [SCT])*

Page 3: An M10 tank destroyer of 20th Anti-Tank Regiment, RA, in action outside the hamlet of la Bijude, 9 July. *(Imperial War Museum [IWM] B6662)*

Page 7: Captain Robert Seaborn of the Canadian Chaplain Service gives absolution to a dying soldier near Caen, 15 July. *(NAC PA-136042)*

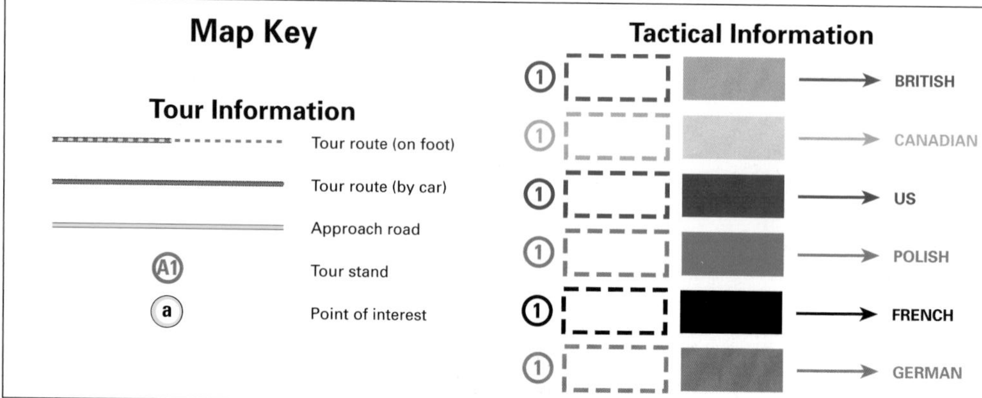

CONTENTS

THE NORMANDY BATTLEFIELD

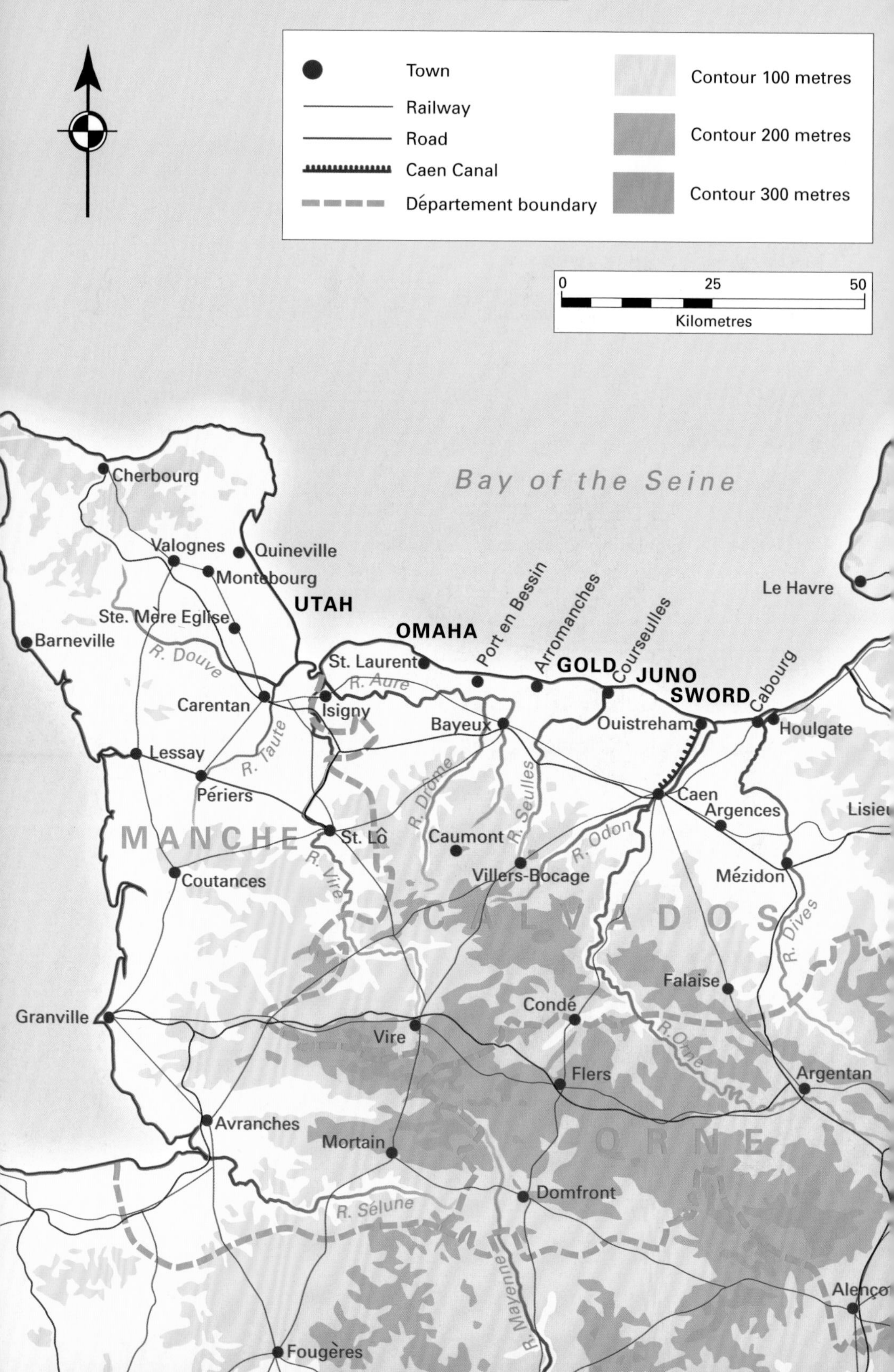

PART ONE

INTRODUCTION

BATTLE ZONE NORMANDY

The Battle of Normandy was one of the greatest military clashes of all time. From late 1943, when the Allies appointed their senior commanders and began the air operations that were such a vital preliminary to the invasion, until the end of August 1944, it pitted against one another several of the most powerful nations on earth, as well as some of their most brilliant minds. When it was won, it changed the world forever. The price was high, but for anybody who values the principles of freedom and democracy, it is difficult to conclude that it was one not worth paying.

I first visited Lower Normandy in 1994, a year after I joined the War Studies Department at the Royal Military Academy Sandhurst (RMAS). With the 50th anniversary of D-Day looming, it was decided that the British Army would be represented at several major ceremonies by one of the RMAS's officer cadet companies. It was also suggested that the cadets should visit some of the battlefields, not least to bring home to them the significance of why they were there. Thus, at the start of June 1994, I found myself as one of a small team of military and civilian directing staff flying with the cadets in a draughty and noisy Hercules transport to visit the beaches and fields of Calvados, in my case for the first time.

I was hooked. Having met some of the veterans and seen the ground over which they fought – and where many of their friends died – I was determined to go back. Fortunately, the Army encourages battlefield touring as part of its soldiers' education, and on numerous occasions since 1994 I have been privileged to return to Normandy, often to visit new sites. In the process I have learned a vast amount, both from my colleagues (several of whom are contributors to this series) and from my enthusiastic and sometimes tri-service audiences, whose professional insights and penetrating questions have frequently made me re-examine my own assumptions and prejudices. Perhaps inevitably, especially when standing in one of Normandy's beautifully-maintained Commonwealth War Graves Commission cemeteries, I have also found myself deeply moved by the critical events that took place there in the summer of 1944.

'Battle Zone Normandy' was conceived by Jonathan Falconer, Commissioning Editor at Sutton Publishing, in 2001. Why not, he suggested, bring together recent academic research – some of which challenges the general perception of what happened on and after 6 June 1944 – with a perspective based on familiarity with the ground itself? We agreed that the opportunity existed for a series that would set out to combine detailed and accurate narratives, based mostly on primary sources, with illustrated guides to the ground itself, which could be used either in the field (sometimes quite literally), or by the armchair explorer. The book in your hands is the product of that agreement.

The 'Battle Zone Normandy' series consists of 14 volumes, covering most of the major and many of the minor engagements that went together to create the Battle of Normandy. The first six books deal with the airborne and amphibious landings on 6 June 1944, and with the struggle to create the firm lodgement that was the prerequisite for eventual Allied victory. Five further volumes cover some of the critical battles that followed, as the Allies' plans unravelled and they were forced to improvise a battle very different from that originally intended. Finally, the last three titles in the series examine the fruits of the bitter attritional struggle of June and July 1944, as the Allies irrupted through the German lines or drove them back in fierce fighting. The series ends, logically enough, with the devastation of the German armed forces in the 'Falaise Pocket' in late August.

Whether you use these books while visiting Normandy, or to experience the battlefields vicariously, we hope you will find them as interesting to read as we did to research and write. Far from the inevitable victory that is sometimes represented, D-Day and the ensuing battles were full of hazards and unpredictability. Contrary to the view often expressed, had the invasion failed, it is far from certain that a second attempt could have been mounted. Remember this, and the significance of the contents of this book, not least for your life today, will be the more obvious.

Dr Simon Trew
Royal Military Academy Sandhurst
December 2003

ACKNOWLEDGEMENTS

With the 'Battle Zone Normandy' series nearing completion, the series editor wants to thank a number of people for making these books possible. At Sutton Publishing, Jeremy Yates-Round, Jim Crawley, Helen Holness and their teams were unfailingly enthusiastic throughout, and did much to maintain the project's momentum to the very end. Jonathan Falconer and Peter Clifford got BZN off the ground in the first place, and provided inspiration and guidance when the size of our task threatened to overwhelm us. Donald Sommerville, Nick Reynolds, Bow Watkinson and Martin Latham met some extremely demanding deadlines with remarkable good humour. Ian and Colin McCarthy at Map Creation, and the indexer Michael Forder were professional throughout, and my sincere thanks go to them too. At the RMAS, support came from the Commandant (Major-General Andrew Ritchie CBE) and Director of Studies (Matthew Midlane), and from my colleagues in the War Studies Department.

Books like this one cannot be written without the help of many individuals and institutions. Simon Trew and Stephen Badsey would particularly like to thank the library staff at Sandhurst under Andrew Orgill. Thanks also to the staffs of the National Archives at Kew, the British Library, the Imperial War Museum and the Public Archives of Canada, plus many regimental and corps museums across the country. Mitchell Yockelson at the US National Archives and Records Administration (NARA) also provided invaluable assistance, and made a research visit in 2002 far more successful than it would otherwise have been.

More personally, the authors want to express their gratitude to family and friends, without whose love and patience *Battle for Caen* could not have appeared. There is simply not the space to name them all here. But special thanks to Helen and Rosie, and to Phylomena, as well as to Michael and Sara Burgun, and to Lt-Col (Ret'd) Michael and Rosemary Chilcott.

This book is dedicated to those who fought and won the Battle of Normandy. Before the last of them depart, the authors want to acknowledge the huge debt that we and our families owe them.

Simon Trew
Stephen Badsey

PART TWO

HISTORY

CHAPTER 1

THE STALEMATE

When British and Canadian troops of Second (British) Army pushed inland from Sword and Juno Beaches on the morning of D-Day, Tuesday 6 June 1944, they could already see in the distance the tallest buildings of Caen, capital of the Calvados *département* (region) of Lower Normandy and the largest town on the Normandy battlefield, its centre only 14 kilometres (km) away. Next day Allied newspapers announced that this vital objective was already falling into their hands. Instead, Caen and its outlying villages became the focus of a stubborn German defence that kept Second Army pinned within sight of the Normandy beaches for the next seven weeks. After attempts to find other ways forward, at the start of July Second Army had no choice but to take Caen and its defences directly. The bitter and hard-fought battle for Caen also played a decisive part in the larger Allied victory in Normandy.

Then and Now

This account describes the battlefield as it was in 1944. Major local differences from the present day are described in the section on battlefield tours. Timings are based on British Double Summer Time (GMT plus two hours) used by the Allies. Caen including its suburbs is much larger than in 1944, with a present population of about 200,000. The northern limits of Caen in 1944 can be traced by the route of the ring-road, but Lébisey Wood has almost vanished, and the eastern suburbs have almost merged together with Giberville, Démouville and Cuverville. Colombelles steelworks was dismantled in the 1980s (and shipped, complete, to China!) although the chimney bases remain, marked on maps as *Anciens hauts fourneaux*. The Caen–Troarn railway line has been removed, although its course can still be traced from the N175 road which follows a broadly parallel route in places only a few metres to the south. The industrial railway line south from Colombelles past Grentheville has also been removed, although its embankment remains. Many small features of the 1944 battlefield, woods, hedges, and orchards including the 'black orchard' west of Troarn no longer exist.

Above: An aerial view of eastern Caen, showing the main railway station (*centre right*), the Canal de Caen (*upper left*) and River Orne (*upper right*). The photo was taken after Allied bombing had damaged much of the city. *(NAC C-104861)*

Page 11: The Sherman Firefly was the best tank available to Second Army. However, only one in four tanks in British and Canadian armoured regiments were Fireflies. Its distinctive long-barrelled gun quickly identified it to the enemy, who prioritised its destruction. *(IWM B7513)*

With a population in 1944 of about 54,000 (compared to 7,000 for nearby Bayeux), Caen originated as a crossing place over the River Orne, which flowed (as it still does) through the town from south-west to north (joined from the west by its tributary the River Odon) to reach the sea at the small port of Ouistreham. The medieval part of Caen was to the north and west of the Orne, with a central citadel mound surrounded by ramparts. Straight roads of Roman origin radiated from this centre like the spokes of wheels, including the main road south to Falaise, and the N13 highway stretching across the Normandy battlefield south-eastward to Paris 240 km away. The direct threat to Paris if the Allies took Caen was obvious to both sides, but it was not enough to capture the town itself; Second Army also had to control enough ground on all sides to ensure that troops and supply convoys could move freely.

The church of St-Pierre in central Caen, seen before the war. *(IWM B8019A)*

The central part of Caen included ancient abbeys, convents and churches, some used as schools or hospitals. The largest churches were close to the citadel mound, including St-Étienne and la Trinité, respectively parts of the Abbaye-aux-Hommes and the Abbaye-aux-Dames ('Men's Abbey' and 'Women's Abbey'), and the renaissance church of St-Pierre. Most of the streets were old and narrow, with stone-built houses clustering all the way up to the citadel ramparts. The only substantial open space was a racecourse on the south side of the town. In the nineteenth century, the Canal de Caen was dug from Ouistreham parallel to the River Orne, and the two waterways together formed a modern docks area, next to the suburb on the east side of Caen called the Faubourg de Vaucelles. Two railway lines met at the main station in Vaucelles: a commercial single-track line from the east past nearby Troarn, and a main line from the south-east and Paris running parallel with the N13 highway and continuing on westward to Cherbourg.

From June 1940 Caen was a centre of German military administration, including the local headquarters of the *Gestapo*, and the dock basins, the railway and the industrial south and east of Caen were all military targets for the Allies. The town was bombed by the Royal Air Force (RAF) in the early hours of D-Day, followed by the US Army Air Force (USAAF) in daylight. Red Cross markers were placed on the roofs of churches, hospitals and refugee centres, but the Allies continued to bomb and shell central Caen intermittently. By late June only the northern part of the town had not been heavily damaged. Many people left Caen or took refuge in the centre, particularly a 'zone of refuge' soon agreed between the Allies and the French Resistance, including the Abbaye-aux-Hommes and the ruins of the convent-hospital of Le Bon Sauveur.

The same building, seen after the capture of Caen. The streets have been cleared of rubble to allow vehicles to pass through the shattered city. *(IWM B8019)*

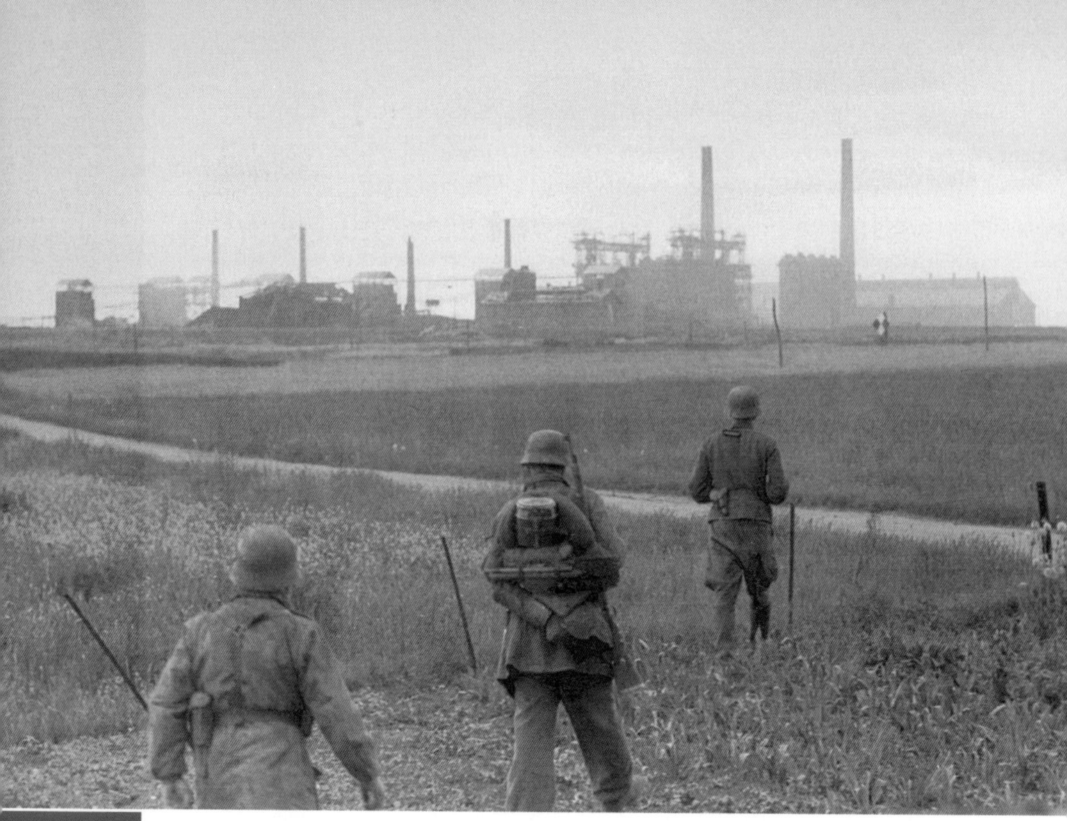

A German patrol moves towards the Colombelles factory area. Some of the tall chimneys used by German observers are visible in the distance. *(Bundesarchiv [BA] 721/353/27a)*

Caen was ringed on all sides by small medieval villages, mostly built around irregular church squares and set back slightly from the road (often just a dirt track), usually with a small manor farmhouse or château. The villages were stone-built with strong walls and deep cellars, many with a church spire that made a good lookout position. Distances between most villages were 1–2 km, lethal range for crossfire from tanks or anti-tank guns in 1944, making them natural fortresses. 'Mopping up' after an attack – clearing the last German sniper or machine-gunner from the last roof or cellar – could take hours or even days. The village and wood of Lébisey just north of Caen marked the furthest penetration towards the town by 3rd British Infantry Division ('The Iron Division') from Sword Beach on D-Day. On the west side of Caen was the village of Carpiquet with a pre-war airfield, l'Aérodrome de Caen-Carpiquet, used by the *Luftwaffe* (German Air Force), a D-Day objective for 3rd Canadian Infantry Division from Juno Beach. To the south-east at the village of Cormelles (the modern Cormelles-le-Royal) was a large car manufacturing plant.

The whitish-yellow limestone of the Caen area provided building material for most of the Calvados region, and the limestone quarries around Caen made good defensive and military storage positions for the Germans. South of Caen along the east side of the Orne valley was a complex of iron-ore mines, with its largest workings south of the village of St-Martin-de-Fontenay; these were known as la Cité de la Mine (described as a 'factory' by the Allies who did not grasp the importance of the mine tunnels to the Germans). The local iron ore fed the steelworks at Colombelles to the east of Caen. The tall factory chimneys (22 before the battle, although many were destroyed in its course) provided excellent observation across the battlefield. An industrial single-track railway line, running south from Colombelles, passed over the main Caen–Paris line on a high embankment just west of the village of Grentheville.

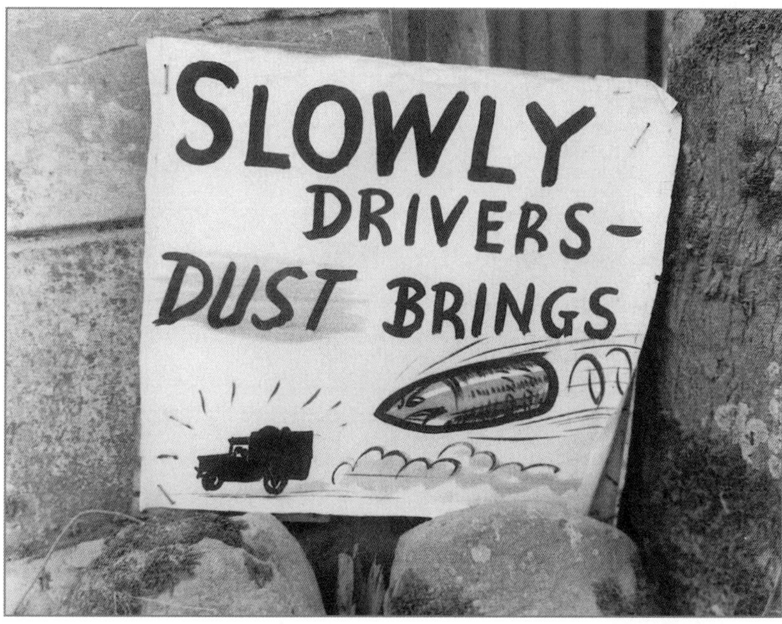

A warning to Second Army personnel not to drive too fast, photographed on 15 July. *(IWM B7431)*

The terrain of the battlefield changed significantly from one side of Caen to another. The well-cultivated farmland soil that overlay the limestone was made of yellowish clay-like loess that turned into a liquid mud in heavy rain and a powdery dust in hot weather. Signs warned that 'Dust Brings Shells' – driving too fast soon brought enemy shelling or mortaring – while on a hot, dry day the combined dust and smoke from shellfire could be as dense as fog.

North of Caen was an area of largely open fields captured by Second Army on D-Day, but to enter Caen from the north meant fighting through the hedges and orchards of the outlying villages, and then the narrow streets of the town itself. South of Caen was the *bocage* or 'hedgerow country', a pattern of small medieval fields and orchards marked by earth banks and foliage. Hill 112 (metres), a large flat-topped promontory emerging out of the hedgerows 10 km to the south-west of Caen between the Odon and the Orne, dominated the area, and was the object of repeated hard fighting in June and July; the Germans called it the *Kalvarienberg* – 'the hill of Calvary'. East of Caen past the canal and the Orne was what the British called the Caen plain, with large walled farms and horse studs. Although open ground compared to the *bocage*, the Caen plain also had its small villages, its orchards, and its fields bounded by strong fences or trees, and the well-grown crops in June and July easily concealed dug-in tanks. East of the narrow Caen plain the ground was *bocage* and marshland breeding mosquitoes that plagued the troops, crossed by numerous small streams and culverts (*ruisseaux*) before rising up as hills including the substantial Bavent Wood (Bois de Bavent). Dominating the area to the south was a long, low and flat-topped ridge 65–85 metres high, called Bourguébus ridge by the British ('Buggers Bus' ridge to most soldiers) and Verrières ridge by the Canadians after two prominent villages. This ridge was the scene of the fighting that finally liberated Caen.

Allied High Command

Supreme Commander Allied Expeditionary Force:
General Dwight D. Eisenhower
Deputy Supreme Commander: Air Chief Marshal Sir Arthur Tedder
Chief of Staff: Lieutenant General Walter Bedell Smith
Commander-in-Chief Allied Naval Expeditionary Force: Adm Sir Bertram Ramsay
Commander Allied Expeditionary Air Force:
Air Chief Marshal Sir Trafford Leigh-Mallory
Commander 21st Army Group: General Sir Bernard L. Montgomery
US First Army: Lieutenant General Omar N. Bradley
Second (British) Army: Lieutenant-General Sir Miles Dempsey

The overall responsibility for Operation Overlord, the Allied plan for victory in North-West Europe, lay with Supreme Headquarters Allied Expeditionary Force (SHAEF) under General Dwight D. Eisenhower, with Air Chief Marshal Sir Arthur Tedder

HISTORY

as his deputy. Planning and command of the land battle in Normandy was entrusted to General Sir Bernard Montgomery commanding 21st Army Group, consisting of First US Army under Lieutenant General Omar N. Bradley and Second (British) Army under Lieutenant-General Sir Miles 'Bimbo' Dempsey. Montgomery's style of command brought him into disagreement with other senior officers, including Tedder. Both during the Normandy fighting and for long afterwards Caen became the focus of this disagreement, precisely because possession of the town was so vital to both sides.

Prime Minister Winston Churchill and General Bernard Montgomery with senior Second Army officers, 22 July. *From left to right:* Lt-Gen G.C. Bucknall (XXX Corps); Lt-Gen N.M. Ritchie (XII Corps); Lt-Gen R.N. O'Connor (VIII Corps); Lt-Gen M.C. Dempsey (Second Army); Lt-Gen J.T. Crocker (I Corps); Lt-Gen G.G. Simonds (II Canadian Corps); Brigadier M.S. Chilton (Dempsey's Chief of Staff). *(IWM B7883)*

Montgomery's plan was for 21st Army Group to assault the beaches of Lower Normandy on D-Day and to push inland. Victory would depend on how fast both sides could build up their reinforcements, supplies and equipment. The Allies hoped to delay German reinforcements from reaching Normandy by a deception scheme code-named Operation 'Fortitude', convincing the Germans that a second and larger landing was coming, probably in the Pas de Calais area; and by using airpower (assisted by sabotage from the French Resistance) to slow the Germans as they moved through France. The critical objectives after D-Day for First US Army were first Cherbourg, and then St-Lô with its important road junction. This meant the Americans fighting through some of the most difficult marsh and *bocage* on the Normandy battlefield. Second Army's role was to threaten a direct break-out south-eastwards past Caen towards Paris, drawing in the German reinforcements, particularly their *Panzer* (armoured) divisions.

Second Army hoped to capture Caen on D-Day or soon after, and the Allies expected to make reasonably steady progress inland in the first month, as far south as Falaise or beyond. The ground gained would provide airfields for the fighter and ground-attack squadrons of RAF Second Tactical Air Force and USAAF Ninth Air Force. An advance deep inland would also provide space to create an additional 12th Army Group under Lt Gen Bradley, composed of First US Army and Third US Army, whereupon Eisenhower and SHAEF would take overall command of the battle, leaving Montgomery in charge of a much smaller 21st Army Group, composed of Second Army and the new First Canadian Army (combining Canadian and British troops under a Canadian commander). Although Montgomery set up his tactical headquarters in Normandy on 8 June, in the grounds of the Château de Creullet (near Creully just inland from Gold and Juno Beaches), SHAEF headquarters remained in England, waiting for Caen to fall.

German High Command

Oberster Befelshaber der Wehrmacht
(Armed Forces Commander-in-Chief): ***Adolf Hitler***

Oberkommando der Wehrmacht (OKW)
(Armed Forces High Command) Chief of Staff:
Generalfeldmarschall Wilhelm Keitel

Oberbefelshaber West (OB West) (Commander-in-Chief West):
Generalfeldmarschall Günther von Kluge

Luftflotte 3 (Third Air Fleet): *Generalfeldmarschall* Hugo Sperrle

Marinegruppenkommando West (Naval Group West):
Admiral Theodore Krancke

Armeegruppe B (Army Gp B): *Generalfeldmarschall* Erwin Rommel

7. Armee (Seventh Army): *SS-Oberstgruppenführer* Paul Hausser

Panzergruppe West (Panzer Gp West):
Gen der Panzertruppen Heinrich Eberbach

Many German commanders in Normandy believed that, once they had failed to stop the Allies on the beaches, they should conduct a fighting withdrawal back to the River Seine. But this strategy was not adopted for various reasons, including a convoluted system of command dominated by Adolf Hitler, who interfered frequently and directly in the battle. The German Army (*Heer*) headquarters responsible for defending France and the Low Countries was *Oberbefelshaber West* (OB West), in Paris. Directly responsible for fighting the battle in Normandy was Army Group B under *Generalfeldmarschall* (Field Marshal) Erwin Rommel, a personal favourite who had direct access to Hitler, with his headquarters at la Roche-Guyon château, 40 km north-west of Paris. Neither OB West nor Army Group B had clear authority over the other German forces in Normandy. The German Navy played little part after D-Day except for a few minor raids on Allied ships. Although the Allies dominated the skies over Normandy, the *Luftwaffe* made some air attacks, usually at dusk or night, and was also responsible for anti-aircraft artillery and even some infantry units. The *Waffen-SS*, the Nazi Party's own fighting force, included some of the most powerful German divisions in Normandy with their own supply and replacement system, and was increasingly favoured by Hitler as suspicions and divisions grew among senior German officers.

Field Marshal Günther von Kluge, OB West from 2 July, was initially optimistic that the Germans could turn the tide in Normandy, but the battle for Caen convinced him otherwise. He committed suicide on 18 August. *(IWM GER 1276)*

Before D-Day, Normandy had been defended by German Seventh Army. On 7 June Panzer Group West was given responsibility for the Caen sector. Although technically subordinate to Seventh Army, in practice it reported directly to Rommel and came to include most of the Panzer divisions in Normandy. In broad terms, from just east of Caen to just west of Bayeux, Panzer Group West opposed Second (British) Army, while Seventh Army, composed mostly of infantry divisions, opposed First US Army in the difficult *bocage* country to the west. Montgomery largely left Bradley and First US Army to fight their own battle, while closely overseeing Dempsey and Second Army's battle for Caen.

In the week after D-Day, Montgomery tried to surround Caen with attacks by I (British) Corps (which included 3rd Canadian Infantry Division) under Lt-Gen J.T. Crocker, but was stalled by counter-attacks from the arriving I SS Panzer Corps under *SS-Obergruppenführer* (Lt-Gen) Josef 'Sepp' Dietrich. The open ground of the Caen plain appeared to be ideal both for an Allied armoured break-out and for a German armoured counter-attack down to the beaches. The Germans kept intense pressure on the bridgehead east of the River Orne, fearing a major attack south-east or east. Rommel also recognised the importance of Cherbourg to the Allies, and at first proposed using infantry divisions to take over the defence of Caen, freeing the Panzers to move into the Cotentin against First US Army. But on 12 June he was over-ruled by Hitler, who ordered Panzer attacks to destroy the Allied beachheads from east to west, starting with the Orne bridgehead, and for all other ground to be held without the possibility of retreat.

With German priorities focused on Cherbourg and Caen, in the second week of June the British and Americans pushed inland in the centre on both sides of Bayeux. While the Americans tried to reach St-Lô, British XXX Corps under Lt-Gen G.C. Bucknall began Operation 'Perch' to get onto Hill 112 from the west, threatening the feared break-out south-eastwards that would force the Germans to give up Caen. Reinforcements from I SS Panzer Corps stopped the British advance at Villers-Bocage on 13 June, followed by more reinforcements from LXVII Panzer Corps, while First US Army's offensive came to a halt north of St-Lô on 18 June. Then, in a month of bad weather, a major storm in the English Channel on 19–21 June delayed the Allied landing timetable by a week.

By 22 June, Second Army had landed some 326,500 men, 57,500 vehicles and 133,500 tons of stores. All these, including fighting divisions, ammunition dumps, hospitals and temporary airstrips had to be fitted into an area barely 40 km wide from the boundary with First US Army to the Orne bridgehead, and from 25 km to barely 7 km deep in front of Caen, where part of Crocker's I Corps faced I SS Panzer Corps, and in the Orne bridgehead where the rest of I Corps faced LXXXVI Corps under *General der Infanterie* (General of Infantry) Hans von Obstfelder. 'If we don't break out soon', went the grim soldiers' joke, 'we'll have to build skyscrapers'.

From D-Day onwards, thousands of aircraft were used to support 21st Army Group's battle, including raids by heavy bombers of USAAF Eighth Air Force or RAF Bomber Command on road or rail targets. But the immediate menace to Panzer Group West came from the Allied fighters and fighter-bombers – *Jabos* to the Germans – and artillery spotters based in Normandy. There was barely room in the beachhead for the Supermarine Spitfires and Hawker Typhoons of Second Tactical Air Force's 83 Group, about half of its squadrons belonging to the Royal Canadian Air Force (RCAF). The best area for new airfields was south of Caen including Bourguébus ridge, which remained in German hands, and the Allied airmen at SHAEF were among the strongest of Montgomery's critics. On 14 June Air Chief Marshal Tedder warned his staff that the failure to expand inland 'had the makings of a dangerous crisis'.

RAF officers in Bayeux assist a group of Benedictine nuns after their evacuation from Caen. The Catholic orders helped the population of Caen by giving them refuge in their religious buildings during the battle for the city. *(IWM CL459)*

German defensive tactics in Normandy were to establish a thin infantry screen as a front line, then after 1–2 km a main battle zone of dug-in infantry with tanks and anti-tank artillery . If taken, these would be shelled by their own side's artillery and mortars from behind a reverse slope, which would also be used as a forming-up position for an armoured counter-attack. The hedgerows and small stone-built villages of Normandy, and some German advantages in weapons, lent themselves to these tactics. Allied infantry had no equivalent of the MG42 'Spandau' belt-fed machine gun, with its high rate of fire. But the big problem was German tank superiority.

The American-built Sherman, the lighter British Cromwell, and the slower-moving and heavily armoured Churchill (used as an infantry support tank) were about equal to the most common German tank, the Panzerkampfwagen IV, nicknamed the *Kochgeschirr* ('mess tin') from its slab-sided appearance. But in most Panzer divisions the tank regiment consisted of a battalion of Panzer IVs plus a battalion of larger Panzer V Panthers with much superior armour and gun power. By early July, Panzer Group West also had three independent battalions of Panzer VI Tiger tanks, almost twice as heavy as a Sherman, and with an 88-mm gun. A shot from a Tiger could penetrate a Sherman's armour from 2 km, while a Sherman needed to get within 200 metres and hit the Tiger's side or rear armour. The Sherman also had a bad reputation for catching fire if hit, and was known as the 'Tommy cooker' or 'Ronson' (from an advert for a cigarette lighter that 'lights first time in all weathers'). Only the up-gunned British Sherman Firefly with a 17-pounder anti-tank gun could take on a Panther with confidence, and even a Tiger with some chance of success. Allied tank crews also feared the highly effective 88-mm Pak 43/41 anti-tank gun (*PanzerAbwehrKanone*), and the *Luftwaffe*'s 88-mm Flak anti-aircraft gun (*FlugAbwehr-Kanone*) which could also be used in an anti-tank role. Between them the near-invulnerable Tiger and the '88' were blamed for many tank losses from less glamorous German weapons, and any unidentified dot on the horizon would make Allied tank crews cautious. The Allied tank response to meeting a Tiger in the open was to reverse quickly and blast it with all available fire-power.

By the end of June, in what was now a battle of attrition, both Second Army and Panzer Group West were running out of trained infantry. For the British (and the all-volunteer Canadian forces) this was because of decisions taken years before on how to allocate the national manpower. Second Army had taken 24,698 casualties, including 3,356 killed, since D-Day; and although 38,000 men had landed as replacements this rate of loss could not be sustained for long. German casualties are harder to determine: OB West returns for June give 35,454 casualties, including 4,975 killed, for the entire Western theatre, while Army Group B listed 62,603 casualties for Normandy alone, both certainly under-estimates. The Germans were forced to use specialists such as engineers or reconnaissance troops as infantry, and 16th *Luftwaffe* Field Division, which arrived in early July to fight in Caen, was composed of aircraftsmen and ground staff converted into combat troops.

The German forces in Normandy relied heavily on *Nebelwerfer* (rocket launcher) units to compensate for their inferiority in conventional artillery. Here troops of 9th Werfer Brigade load a camouflaged 150-mm *Nebelwerfer* east of Caen. *(BA 299/1821/27a)*

The exact German forces involved in the fighting for Caen are often disputed, partly through their combining of troops from different divisions and even battalions into battlegroups, and partly through difficulties in identifying their strength on a given day. From apparently typical figures, it seems that German infantry and tank battalions by the start of July fought at slightly more than half the strength of their Allied equivalents. The Germans relied on extra fire-power from attached artillery, mortar and anti-tank units to strengthen their divisions, especially the multi-barrelled *Nebelwerfer* ('smoke projector' from its original function) rocket launcher of various calibres, known from its distinctive sound as the 'Moaning Minnie' by the British, and by French-speaking Canadians as *la Vache* ('the cow'). Many German divisions had a *Nebelwerfer* unit attached to their artillery, and British and Canadian infantry estimated that 70 per cent of their casualties in June and July came from rocket and mortar fire. Many such wounds were slight and the victims returned to fight after first-aid, but the effects of shock and the sudden loss of men were considerable.

Allied airfields in Normandy required large areas of flat, open ground. The need for sufficient space for such facilities put considerable pressure on Montgomery to capture Caen and the plateau further south. *(NAC PA-129123)*

To compensate for its shortage of infantry and weakness in tanks, Second Army's fighting methods required building up reserves for about a week and then unleashing what Montgomery called a 'colossal crack' against part of the German line. For each corps of Second Army there was an Army Group Royal Artillery (AGRA), usually of one heavy and three medium artillery regiments. For big attacks the infantry divisions were supported by an attached armoured brigade of three battalions (with confusing terminology, British tank battalions were called 'regiments', and armoured brigades with Churchills were called 'tank' brigades). Overwhelming air and artillery fire-power supported these combined infantry and armoured attacks on a narrow frontage to a limited depth, typically made by one infantry brigade leading and other brigades being fed through, fighting through the main German battle positions and then going into defence to destroy the expected tank counter-attack by using towed or self-propelled anti-tank guns. Armoured divisions were meant chiefly for exploitation, and were organised into an armoured brigade of three tank battalions plus an infantry battalion in half-tracks, and an infantry brigade in lorries, plus an armoured reconnaissance battalion. Between each big attack smaller operations continued to secure important ground. The sheer weight of air and artillery fire-power available to the Allies stunned German commanders and soldiers alike. The Typhoon fighter-bomber with its salvo of eight 60-pound unguided rockets was particularly feared, and some German crews would abandon their tanks if attacked by one. But, like the high-quality British and Canadian artillery, the aircraft could smother an area with fire but might not hit a critical target. Just as mortars might cause only slight wounds, so airpower and artillery usually damaged tanks rather than destroying them, and they could often be repaired quickly. Montgomery's progress by these methods was slow, and an increasing source of concern for SHAEF and Eisenhower.

On 17 June Hitler travelled to Margival (near Soissons, the closest that he came to the Normandy battlefield), to hear arguments from his generals that Army Group B should fall back, which he rejected. On 18 June Montgomery issued his own new orders: to continue the battle of attrition but to capture both Cherbourg and Caen quickly. Cherbourg fell to the Americans on 27 June and First US Army, growing in strength with plenty of reserves, could turn its full force southwards. The big British offensive to take Caen began after the Channel storm, on 26 June, using the new VIII Corps under Lt-Gen Sir Richard O'Connor. Named Operation 'Epsom', this was a large-scale attack through the *bocage* and across the Odon towards Hill 112. It took most of six Panzer divisions to stop Epsom short of its final objectives, five of them *Waffen-SS* including the newly-arrived II SS Panzer Corps (9th SS Panzer Division *Hohenstaufen* and 10th SS Panzer Division *Frundsberg*), which had been intended to be part of a decisive counter-attack.

The failure of their counter-attack plans and an evidently lost battle brought about a crisis in German command in Normandy. On 28 June the general commanding Seventh Army committed suicide; he was replaced by the commander of II SS Panzer Corps, *SS-Oberstgruppenführer* (General) Paul Hausser, significantly the first time that a *Waffen-SS* officer had been given such a senior Army command. By 2 July OB West also had a new commander, Field Marshal Günther von Kluge, followed by a new commander for Panzer Group West on 6 July, *General der Panzertruppen* (General of Armoured Troops) Heinrich Eberbach. Only Rommel remained at Army Group B; and Hitler did not know that Rommel, convinced that the war was lost, was already involved on the fringes of a plot to assassinate him. The tensions and suspicions among senior

German officers produced an atmosphere in which all motives and statements became suspect.

On the Allied side, blame for the failure to advance inland tended to focus lower down, with demands for divisional and battalion commanders to push their men harder, and claims that veteran troops had become battle-weary. On 30 June, the last of the four British corps of Second Army, XII Corps under Lt-Gen N.M. Ritchie, was activated. Within the next two weeks Second Army would reach its greatest strength before declining owing to the shortage of infantry. V-1 'flying bombs' had first begun to hit London on 14 June, and there were increasing demands for an advance along the Channel coast to capture their launch sites. On 3 July, Lt Gen Bradley began his new offensive southward with First US Army, attacking continuously along one part of the front after another; but because of the difficult terrain the offensive made limited progress and was halted by 15 July, replaced by a slow grind to secure St-Lô.

By this time British military intelligence, including the famous 'Ultra' code-breaking system, had identified fresh German infantry divisions joining Panzer Group West, enabling one armoured division – the Panzer Lehr Division – to move across to First US Army's front, to join 2nd SS Panzer Division *Das Reich* and 17th SS Panzergrenadier Division *Götz von Berlichingen*. The Fortitude deception could not last forever, criticism of Montgomery continued to mount especially at SHAEF headquarters, and by any calculation the fall of Caen was long overdue. With no space to deploy in the Orne bridgehead to the east, and no further way forward through the *bocage* past the Odon to the west, the only remaining choice for Montgomery was to hit Caen head-on. On 30 June he issued orders for Second Army to take Caen, 'and the sooner the better'.

CHAPTER 2

THE LIBERATION OF CAEN

On Tuesday 4 July, in the week between Operation Epsom and the next big attack by Second Army, a small preliminary battle, code-named Operation 'Windsor', took place to the west of Caen and gave a good indication of the bitter fighting to come. 3rd Canadian

3rd Canadian Infantry Division played a central role in the battle for Caen. These are some of the division's senior officers, photographed on 25 June. *Front row, from second left to right* Brigadier R.A. Wyman (commander 2nd Canadian Armoured Brigade, supporting the division); Brigadier H.W. Foster (commander 7th Infantry Brigade); Maj-Gen. R.F.L. Keller (division commander); Lt-Gen. J.T. Crocker (commander British I Corps, to which the division was subordinated); Brigadier. P.A.S. Todd (divisional artillery commander); Brigadier K.G. Blackader (commander 8th Infantry Brigade); Brigadier. D.G. Cunningham (commander 9th Infantry Brigade). *(NAC PA-129038)*

Infantry Division under Major-General (Maj-Gen) 'Rod' Keller, which had been fighting since D-Day, was to capture Carpiquet village and aerodrome with a reinforced infantry brigade, supported by a phenomenal weight of fire-power. Including the battleship HMS *Rodney* (nine 16-inch guns) and the monitor HMS *Roberts* (two 15-inch guns), 760 guns fired the opening barrage for Operation Windsor, and 428 guns fired 30,250 shells in support of the brigade during the day.

Carpiquet had eluded the Canadians since D-Day and, like the rest of the western outskirts of Caen, it was defended mainly by troops of 12th SS Panzer Division *Hitlerjugend*, commanded by *SS-Brigadeführer* (roughly equivalent to Brigadier) Kurt Meyer (known to his troops as 'Panzermeyer'). The *Hitlerjugend* ('Hitler Youth') Division had been recruited from 17–18 year-olds who had grown up as devout Nazis, commanded by combat veterans, and had been in action since 7 June, often against the Canadians. The hangars and control tower at Carpiquet were protected by *Luftwaffe* concrete bunkers, and defended by 1st Battalion, 26th SS Panzer-grenadier Regiment (I/26th SS Panzergrenadiers) dug in among the hangars along the southern edge of the runway, with a reinforced company to the north in Carpiquet village. About 2 km south in the Odon valley, including the village of Verson, was II/1st SS Panzergrenadiers from 1st SS Panzer Division *Leibstandarte Adolf Hitler* under *SS-Obergruppenführer* (Lt-Gen) 'Teddy' Wisch.

A Sherman tank of the Fort Garry Horse photographed by the wrecked northern hangars at Carpiquet airfield. *(NAC PA-169311)*

The preliminaries to Operation Windsor began late on 3 July when the British 214th Infantry Brigade of 43rd (Wessex) Division in neighbouring VIII Corps occupied Fontaine-Étoupefour, while next morning one squadron of Shermans from the Sherbrooke Fusiliers (Canadian 27th Armoured Regiment) made a diversion to the north towards Gruchy. At 0515 hours on 4 July, before dawn in bad weather, 8th Canadian Infantry Brigade attacked Carpiquet from the west behind the artillery and air bombardment. The *Waffen-SS* replied by concentrating artillery, mortars and machine guns from both flanks onto the attacking Canadians. By 0930 hours Le Régiment de la Chaudière and the North Shore Regiment together with Shermans of the Fort Garry Horse (10th Armoured Regiment) had captured Carpiquet village from its *Hitlerjugend* garrison. To the south the Royal Winnipeg Rifles with a squadron of Fort Garry Horse and British Crocodile flame-throwing tanks of 141st Regiment, Royal Armoured Corps (141st RAC) had a much harder fight. They reached the main hangar positions by 0800 hours but were driven back almost to their start line, taking flanking fire from II/1st SS Panzergrenadiers from positions north of Verson. Rather than surrender, even to the flame-throwers, the *Waffen-SS* boy-soldiers hid in their bunkers and then emerged expecting to kill or be killed. The remaining Canadian battalion, the Queen's Own Rifles of Canada, moved up to Carpiquet village, intending to capture the control tower complex at the eastern end of the runway, but was also unable to advance any further. Resuming the attack at about 1600 hours, the Royal Winnipeg Rifles again reached the south-west hangar area, but fell back as the Panthers of I/12th SS Panzers approached from the east. By 2100 hours the Winnipeg Rifles were back behind their start line, leaving only Carpiquet village and the northern part of the airfield in Canadian hands. The Panthers were attacked by rocket fire from a wing of 44 Typhoons, and the control tower area was shelled by the 16-inch guns of HMS *Rodney*.

During the night, I/1st SS Panzergrenadiers led a counter-attack to recapture Carpiquet village from the north that was not finally beaten off until 0800 hours next day. Also on 5 July British patrols fell back from Verson, and the Canadians were left holding Carpiquet village under German shellfire and frequent counter-attacks from three sides. After the battle, both Lt-Gen Crocker and Lt-Gen Dempsey pressed, without success, to have Maj-Gen Keller removed from command of his division.

Both sides in Normandy were well aware that fighting house-to-house involved almost total destruction of the area concerned, would use up large numbers of troops, and result in staggering loss of life. The Germans also knew from prisoners and signals intelligence that Caen was about to be attacked. From 29 June onwards their administrative troops and staff were pulled out, including the *Gestapo*. Residents also began to abandon the northern part of the town and by 7 July only about 20,000 civilians still remained in Caen, many in the zone of refuge and the abbeys.

For both OKW and Rommel the most important thing was to preserve the Panzer divisions. On 1–2 July, the under-trained 16th *Luftwaffe* Field Division arrived at Caen and began taking over the eastern part and the outlying villages on either side of the Orne, including Lébisey and Colombelles, from 21st Panzer Division which left I/22nd Panzers behind in support (with Panzer IVs – the division was unusual in having no Panther battalion). But 271st Infantry Division, intended to relieve the *Hitlerjugend* Division west and north of Caen, was still in transit together with 272nd Infantry Division, and the *Waffen-SS* troops had to remain in place.

On 5 July Second Army issued orders for Operation 'Charnwood' to start at 0420 hours (90 minutes before dawn) on Saturday 8 July, using three divisions of Lt-Gen Crocker's I Corps to converge from the north into the centre of Caen and as far south as the line of the River Odon and the River Orne, securing bridges across both rivers. As Dempsey explained on 7 July, Second Army was required, 'to draw to itself and contain the maximum number of German divisions; to hold the present front; and when opportunity offers, to take Caen'. Charnwood was a Montgomery-style 'set-piece' battle in five phases, each phase only starting on orders from I Corps headquarters. 3rd British Infantry Division would attack on a one-brigade front from the north-east towards Lébisey, with 33rd Armoured Brigade in reserve; the fresh 59th (Staffordshire) Division would attack on a two-brigade front from the north on both sides of the Basly road (the modern D79) from just south of Cambes-en-Plaine, supported by 27th Armoured Brigade; and 3rd Canadian Infantry Division would attack on a one-brigade front from the north-west down the Cairon road (the modern D22) with 2nd Canadian Armoured Brigade, through the outlying villages of Buron, Gruchy and Authie and then eastwards into Caen.

The artillery support for Operation Charnwood came from two AGRAs and the field guns of five divisions, about 400 guns. The German positions were also well within range of British warships offshore: HMS *Rodney*, HMS *Roberts*, and the cruisers HMS *Belfast* (twelve 6-inch guns) and HMS *Emerald* (seven 6-inch guns). The new idea for Charnwood was to use massed heavy bombers, the Avro Lancasters and Handley Page Halifaxes of RAF Bomber Command, to blast a way through the German positions. This was the first attempt in Normandy to co-ordinate heavy bombers with a major ground attack, and their use reflected an increasing Allied readiness to try anything to break the Caen deadlock. Bomber

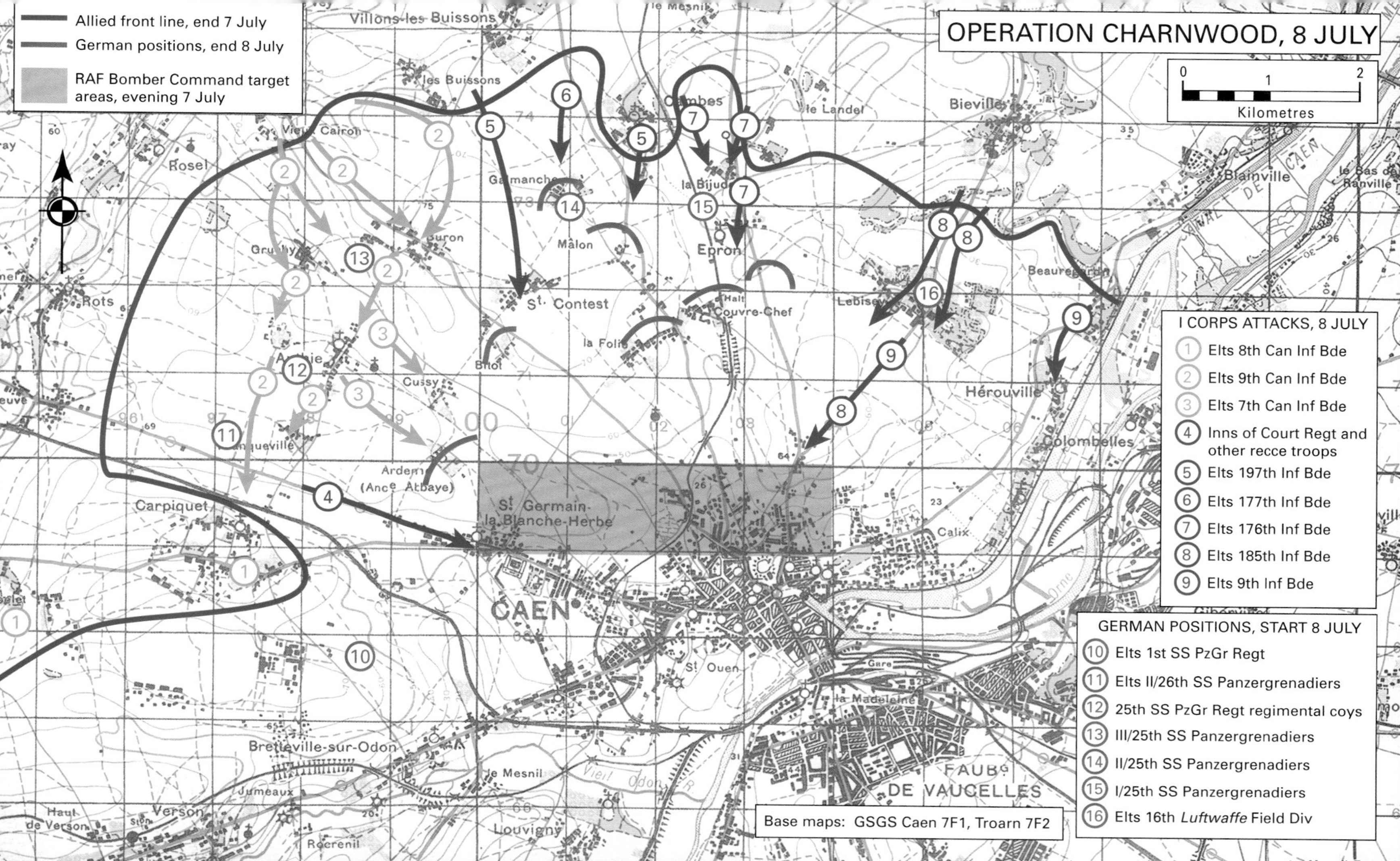

OPERATION CHARNWOOD, 8 JULY
0
1
2
Kilometres
Allied front line, end 7 July
German positions, end 8 July
RAF Bomber Command target areas, evening 7 July
I CORPS ATTACKS, 8 JULY
1 Elts 8th Can Inf Bde
2 Elts 9th Can Inf Bde
3 Elts 7th Can Inf Bde
4 Inns of Court Regt and other recce troops
5 Elts 197th Inf Bde
6 Elts 177th Inf Bde
7 Elts 176th Inf Bde
8 Elts 185th Inf Bde
9 Elts 9th Inf Bde
GERMAN POSITIONS, START 8 JULY
10 Elts 1st SS PzGr Regt
11 Elts II/26th SS Panzergrenadiers
12 25th SS PzGr Regt regimental coys
13 III/25th SS Panzergrenadiers
14 II/25th SS Panzergrenadiers
15 I/25th SS Panzergrenadiers
16 Elts 16th *Luftwaffe* Field Div
Base maps: GSGS Caen 7F1, Troarn 7F2
Villons-les-Buissons
les Buissons
Rosel
Rots
Buron
Malon
Epron
la Bijude
le Landel
Bieville
Blainville
CANAL DE CAEN
le Bas de Ranville
Beauregard
Lebisey
Hérouville
Colombelles
St. Contest
Couvre-Chef
la Folie
Bitot
Cussy
Authie
Ardenne (Ance Abbaye)
Carpiquet
St Germain-la-Blanche-Herbe
CAEN
Calix
St Ouen
Gare
la Madeleine
FAUBG DE VAUCELLES
Bretteville-sur-Odon
le Mesnil
Jumeaux
Verson
Haut de Verson
Louvigny
Rocreuil
Orne

A dug-in Panzer IV of I/22nd Panzer Regiment, photographed near Lébisey after being knocked out during Operation Charnwood. *(IWM B7056)*

Command support had to be requested by Second Army through SHAEF in England, and the airmen gained the impression that bombing was needed to destroy major concrete bunker defensive systems in northern Caen. Such bunkers did exist but not on any scale, and Second Army intelligence estimates showed only weak German defences south of the outer ring of villages.

Area bombing was as random as it was powerful; the British were bombing civilians that they had come to liberate, and there was a strong risk of hitting their own troops as well. As a result, the bombing plan was very safety-conscious. Bomber Command's target was 'four grid squares' (squares equal to 1,000 metres across on British military maps), in fact a box 4 km across with its forward edge set 6 km south of the British and Canadian front-line positions and an expected creep-back depth of 1–1.5 km, placing it across most of northern Caen and its outskirts. The area to be bombed was also to the north of the zone of refuge in central Caen. As an extra precaution the bombing would take place late in the evening before the battle, with 15 per cent of the bombs delay-fused to explode coinciding with the ground attack over six hours later.

The British knew that the *Hitlerjugend* Division and 16th *Luftwaffe* Division had taken up a forward defence among the villages north of Caen, but not that there was almost nothing behind them, and that they were very thinly stretched. The boundary between the divisions was near the main road (the modern D7) north out of Caen. The *Hitlerjugend*'s tank strength on 7 July was 24 Panthers of I/12th SS Panzers and 37 Panzer IVs of II/12th SS Panzers. The main defence line was held by 25th SS Panzergrenadiers, deployed in a 9-km arc of villages from the north-east round to the west. I/25th SS Panzergrenadiers was on both sides of the main road, including the hamlet of la Bijude just south-east of Cambes-en-Plaine. There was then a gap before II/25th SS Panzergrenadiers' positions defending Galmanche with nine Panzer IVs, then another gap to III/25th SS Panzergrenadiers' positions in front of Buron. Just north of the N13 road, St-Louet château and Franqueville were defended by a mix of 25th SS Panzergrenadiers' reconnaissance, flak and engineer companies. The weak II/26th SS Panzergrenadiers held the remaining front from Franqueville southwards to the Odon valley, supported by five Panzer IVs and the 88-mm guns of 2nd and 3rd Batteries, 12th SS Flak Battalion (2/ and 3/12th SS Flak). At least seven Panthers of I/12th SS Panzers also remained at Bretteville-sur-Odon. Most of the divisional artillery had pulled back across the Orne to Vaucelles, except for 12th SS Werfer Battalion and the attached 83rd Werfer Regiment. 25th SS Panzergrenadier headquarters was at Ardennes Abbey, just north of St-Germain-la-Blanche-Herbe, with the divisional reserve of 17 Panthers from I/12th SS Panzers. For counter-attacks a group of 23 Panzer IVs of II/12th SS Panzers was held on the western edge of Caen, and III/26th SS Panzergrenadiers on the north-western edge (I/26th SS Panzergrenadiers was out of the line south of Caen, along with other units). The *Hitlerjugend* headquarters had been moved from Ardennes Abbey to the Abbaye-aux-Dames in the town centre.

16th *Luftwaffe* Division's dispositions are less certain. Its front from west of Lébisey and its nearby wood through Hérouville to the Canal de Caen appears to have been held by the two battalions of 31st *Luftwaffe* Rifles (*Luftwaffe-Jäger*) and the divisional fusilier battalion, with the rest of the division deployed east of the Orne or still arriving. The German deployment reflected the reality that they would fight hard for long enough to fulfil the spirit of Hitler's no-retreat order and then pull back out of Caen if they could, sacrificing the *Luftwaffe* troops to preserve the *Waffen-SS*.

British and Commonwealth heavy bombers were used in large numbers for the opening phases of Charnwood and Goodwood. This Handley Page Halifax of 429 Squadron, RCAF, is pictured over the outskirts of Caen on 18 July. With its entire starboard tailplane smashed away, it crashed in the target area. *(IWM)*

On the late afternoon of 7 July, the 16-inch guns of HMS *Rodney* fired repeated salvos at Point 64, the junction of the roads from Lébisey and Épron just north of the outskirts of Caen (this junction no longer exists because of modern road building), seen as the key to the defences, followed by a rocket strike by Typhoons at 2100 hours near Buron. The RAF bombing started at 2150 hours with a force of 467 Lancasters and Halifaxes from 1, 4 and 6 (RCAF) Groups led by Lancasters and Mosquitoes of 8 (Pathfinder) Group approaching from the north in the loose 'gaggle' formation used by Bomber Command for daylight area bombing, flying at just over 1,000 metres, the effective ceiling of German light flak. The Pathfinders released their target markers, followed by 2,562 tons of bombs, two-thirds of them 1,000-lb (500-kg) high explosive, the remainder 500-lb high explosive; flak was light, and only three Lancasters and one Mosquito were lost. At 2250 hours a second wave of six squadrons of Mosquito light bombers from Second Tactical Air Force's 2 Group arrived to bomb point targets. By last light the area of northern Caen under the bombing had been reduced to rubble and overlapping bomb craters. About 400 French civilians died, many others were injured. As hoped by Second Army, all but one of the roads south through Caen were blocked, hampering the German withdrawal and cutting off any reinforcements. But the bombing box largely missed both the defended villages and the German counter-attack reserves further south in Caen. Tanks were hit and temporarily disabled, but in the *Hitlerjugend* Division only two Panzer IVs were destroyed outright.

The youngsters of 25th SS Panzergrenadier Regiment fought desperately to halt Operation Charnwood, and paid a heavy price in doing so. Here one of them lies dead near Mâlon on 9 July. *(IWM B6807)*

Starting at 2300 hours, I Corps artillery blasted the outlying villages throughout the night, supported by the big naval guns. The artillery then laid down a rolling barrage to lead off the infantry attack at 0420 hours on 8 July. At 0700 hours, in daylight under a cloudy sky, four groups of B-26 Marauder medium bombers of Ninth Air Force made a second attack on Caen. There were no aircraft losses, but with a battle happening underneath them the Americans were under orders not to bomb unless certain of their targets, which were partially obscured by cloud. Only 87 out of 192 aircraft released their bombs, and a further 133 tons fell across Caen. Some bombs fell very wide, and a few damaged the *Hitlerjugend* headquarters at the Abbaye-aux-Dames.

Phase one of Operation Charnwood started on time at 0420 hours as the British troops and tanks advanced through trampled wheatfields towards the German defensive screen. Some of the northern villages lay surrounded by woods and by thick hedges and banks, and all were hidden by the dust and smoke of the barrage. 185th Infantry Brigade led the attack by 3rd British Infantry Division under Maj-Gen 'Bolo' Whistler, supported by Shermans of the Staffordshire Yeomanry. 1st Royal Norfolks joined 2nd Royal Warwicks in attacking Lebisey village and wood, while further east 2nd Lincolns (9th Infantry Brigade) attacked Herouville (now part of Herouville-St-Clair). There was heavy fighting at Herouville, but Lebisey was cleared within an hour, although the Germans continued to hold the southern edge of the dense Lebisey wood.

The bombing of Caen on 7 July caused widespread destruction in the city. Here, a patrol struggles along a rubble-choked street three days later. *(NAC PA-116510)*

Also at 0420 hours, 59th (Staffordshire) Division attacked with 2nd/6th South Staffords west of the Caen road aiming to capture Galmanche and its surrounding wood, while east of the road 176th Infantry Brigade led by 6th North Staffords aimed for la Bijude. As the first reports of success arrived, Lt-Gen Crocker ordered phase two for the division to start at 0730 hours, with 176th Infantry Brigade being joined by 197th Infantry Brigade to press forward to the next line of villages. This was also the start time for 3rd Canadian Infantry Division to join in from the west.

There was a good view of the fight for Lébisey from the chimneys of Colombelles steelworks, and at about 0900 hours *General* Eberbach of Panzer Group West arrived at the *Hitlerjugend* headquarters to enquire about help for 16th *Luftwaffe* Division against 3rd British Infantry Division's attack. In a reflection of command relationships between the *Heer* and the *Waffen-SS*, he was turned down by Panzermeyer, who was two ranks his junior. At 1015 hours Eberbach ordered *General* von Obstfelder, commanding LXXXVI Corps, to send 21st Panzer Division's remaining Panzer IV battalion, II/22nd Panzers, across the canal into Caen to support the *Luftwaffe* troops, but despite being repeated the order could not be carried out due to the devastation from the bombing. Directed by spotter aircraft, the Royal Navy continued to hit Point 64 and other key positions, and the guns of HMS *Rodney* broke up a group of 35 tanks assembling 4 km south of Caen near the Falaise road at the village of Ifs, possibly II/22nd Panzers looking for a way through. During the afternoon II/22nd Panzers and two companies of I/192nd Panzergrenadiers crossed the Canal de Caen at Mondeville to support 31st *Luftwaffe* Rifles.

Phase two began for 3rd British Infantry Division at 1100 hours after a considerable time mopping up the German positions in Lébisey Wood, with 2nd King's Shropshire Light Infantry (2nd KSLI) taking over 185th Infantry Brigade's advance and 33rd Armoured Brigade coming under the divisional command. The morning's fight had broken the resistance of 31st *Luftwaffe* Rifles, and 3rd British Infantry Division secured its phase two objectives shortly after midday, pushing its armour and 2nd East Yorkshires from its reserve 8th Infantry Brigade to the west to help 59th (Staffordshire) Division. Thereafter the I Corps phase plan became unnecessary, as German resistance was limited to harassment by snipers and mortar fire. By 1600 hours, 2nd KSLI had captured Point 64 overlooking Caen almost without loss. This was 185th

Allied Order of Battle for Operation Charnwood

Second (British) Army — ***Lt-Gen Sir Miles Dempsey***

3rd Army Group Royal Artillery; 4th Army Group Royal Artillery

79th Armoured Division (part) — ***Maj-Gen Sir Percy Hobart***

22nd Dragoons (Crab flail tanks);
141st Regiment RAC (Crocodile flame-throwing tanks);
5th Assault Regiment Royal Engineers (AVREs)

I Corps — ***Lt-Gen J.T. Crocker***

3rd British Infantry Division — ***Maj-Gen L.G. Whistler***

8th Infantry Brigade:
1st Suffolk Regt; 2nd East Yorks Regt; 1st South Lancs Regt

9th Infantry Brigade:
2nd Lincolnshire Regt; 1st King's Own Scottish Borderers;
2nd Royal Ulster Rifles

185th Infantry Brigade:
2nd Royal Warwickshire Regt; 1st Royal Norfolk Regt;
2nd King's Shropshire Light Infantry

3rd Recce Regt RAC; 2nd Middlesex Regt (MG)
7th, 33rd, 76th Field Regts RA; 20th AT Regt RA; 20th LAA Regt RA

Attached
33rd Armoured Brigade:
1st Northamptonshire Yeomanry; 144th & 148th Regiments, RAC
from 27th Armoured Brigade:
The Staffordshire Yeomanry

3rd Canadian Division — ***Maj-Gen R.F.L. Keller***

7th Canadian Infantry Brigade:
Royal Winnipeg Rifles; Regina Rifles Regt; 1st Canadian Scottish Regt

8th Canadian Infantry Brigade:
Queen's Own Rifles of Canada; Le Régiment de la Chaudière;
North Shore (New Brunswick) Regt

9th Canadian Infantry Brigade:
HLI of Canada; Stormont, Dundas & Glengarry Highlanders;
North Nova Scotia Highlanders

17th Duke of York's Royal Canadian Hussars (7th Recce Regt);
1st Cameron Highlanders of Ottawa (MG)
12th, 13th, 14th Field Regts RCA; 3rd AT Regt RCA; 4th LAA Regt RCA

Attached
2nd Canadian Armoured Brigade:
1st Hussars (6th Armd Regt); Fort Garry Horse (10th Armd Regt);
Sherbrooke Fusiliers (27th Armd Regt)

Also attached
The Inns of Court (Reconnaissance) Regiment;
245 and 247 Btys, 62nd AT Regiment RA

59th (Staffordshire) Division ***Maj-Gen L.O. Lyne***

176th Infantry Brigade:
7th Royal Norfolk Regt; 7th South Staffordshire Regt; 6th North Staffordshire Regt

177th Infantry Brigade:
5th South Staffordshire Regt; 1st/6th South Staffordshire Regt; 2nd/6th South Staffordshire Regt

197th Infantry Brigade:
1st/7th Royal Warwickshire Regt; 2nd/5th Lancashire Fusiliers; 5th East Lancashire Regt

50th Recce Regt RAC; 7th Royal Northumberland Fusiliers (MG)
61st, 110th, 116th Field Regts RA; 68th AT Regt RA; 68th LAA Regt RA

Attached
27th Armoured Brigade:
13th/18th Royal Hussars; 1st East Riding Yeomanry
(less The Staffordshire Yeomanry attached to 3rd Br Inf Div)

Also attached
248th Self-Propelled Bty, 62nd AT Regiment, RA (M10s)

A 6-pounder anti-tank gun of 1st King's Own Scottish Borderers guards a street in central Caen, with two artillery observation tanks behind it. St-Pierre church is in the background. *(IWM B6924)*

Infantry Brigade's objective on D-Day and it had taken 32 days to reach. At 1700 hours, 9th Infantry Brigade took over the advance and patrols, riding on tanks from 33rd Armoured Brigade, moved southwards into the town, held up largely by the bomb craters and the mountains of rubble filling the streets.

Phase two went badly for 59th Division. As 2nd/5th Lancashire Fusiliers advanced towards Mâlon, 1st/7th Warwicks towards St-Contest, and 7th Norfolks towards Épron at 0730 hours, the *Hitlerjugend* troops began emerging from parts of Galmanche and la Bijude which had not been properly cleared, retaking the hamlets and reoccupying a trench system between them, while some Panzer IVs from Buron moved east in support. The attack turned into a protracted battle in which II/25th SS Panzergrenadiers resisted every means used, including flame-throwing and petard mortar tanks, to clear them out of the villages. By nightfall 59th Division remained hung up in the German battle zone, holding St-Contest, la Bijude and Épron, but not Mâlon and Galmanche, although the bombing had blocked or deterred any major German counter-attack.

3rd Canadian Infantry Division joined in at phase two at 0730 hours with the Stormont Dundas and Glengarry Highlanders (the Glens) and the Highland Light Infantry (HLI) of Canada from 9th Canadian Infantry Brigade attacking southwards behind another formidable barrage. Gruchy fell soon after 0930 after a mounted charge by the Bren carriers of the 17th Duke of York's Royal Canadian Hussars (7th Reconnaissance Regiment). Buron (later known to the Canadians as 'Bloody Buron') was a much harder fight that went on all day, although the Canadians successfully fought off the Panzer counter-attacks.

At 0955 hours Maj-Gen Keller ordered phase three for 3rd Canadian Division, but German resistance remained strong and it was not until 1530 hours that phase two was completed, by 9th Canadian Infantry Brigade's reserve battalion, the North Nova Scotia Highlanders, being fed through southwards to capture Authie, while the Glens captured the nearby St-Louet château. The Germans were seen pulling out southwards from Carpiquet aerodrome and the Canadians quickly followed up by capturing Franqueville. The Canadian line now turned to face almost due east towards Ardennes Abbey and Cussy village.

Phase three began at 1830 hours as 7th Canadian Infantry Brigade was fed through eastward towards Caen. Sepp Dietrich at I SS Panzer Corps headquarters radioed Panzermeyer that, 'If you

British infantry set off through thigh-high crops at the start of Operation Charnwood. *(IWM B6618)*

are thrown back to the southern banks of the Orne while fighting a superior enemy, it could never be considered to be a withdrawal contrary to orders', and this was taken as permission to retreat. After a counter-attack led by Panthers failed, Cussy fell to the 1st Canadian Scottish at about 2030 hours. The defence of Ardennes Abbey was organised by Meyer personally, using the remaining Panthers and a few troops from III/1st SS Panzergrenadiers, and although the Regina Rifles got right up to the walls of the abbey, the fight there continued into the small hours. Scout cars of the Inns of Court Regiment (a British reconnaissance unit temporarily with the Canadians) got eastward along the main Bayeux–Caen road as far as St-Germain-la-Blanche-Herbe, and by nightfall the front line of 3rd Canadian Infantry Division was about 4 km from 3rd British Infantry Division, the width of the rubble-filled bombing box. Although the *Hitlerjugend* troops had held 59th (Staffordshire) Division, they were in real danger of being surrounded.

During the night patrols from 3rd British Infantry Division made contact with the Inns of Court Regiment scout cars at St-Germain-la-Blanche-Herbe, as Germans from both defending divisions started to extract themselves through Caen, mainly eastwards into the Orne bridgehead rather than south. Shortly before midnight 21st Panzer Division was ordered by LXXXVI Corps to assemble a battlegroup south of Hérouville and recapture Point 64, but this was abandoned when it was learned that the *Hitlerjugend* Division was retreating. By 0400 hours Meyer's headquarters was in its new position across the Orne. The heavy weapons of II SS Panzer Corps, I SS Panzer Corps and LXXXVI Corps supporting Caen were also pulled back.

For 9 July, 59th Division was ordered to clear its existing positions and advance a mere 200–300 metres to the next line of villages and farms, Couvrechef, la Folie and Bitot, while 3rd Canadian and 3rd British Infantry Divisions closed the encirclement of Caen from west and east to the line of the Orne. At 0200 hours, Battlegroup *Rauch* of 192nd Panzergrenadiers moved across into Caen to cover the retreat of the remaining tanks of 22nd Panzers; the British were unaware of any attack being made. By midday 33rd Armoured Brigade had captured Couvrechef for 59th (Staffordshire) Division, sending patrols southwards. At 0925 hours, 9th Infantry Brigade started its own advance southwards, working its way past piles of rubble over three metres high in the face of the snipers and mortar teams left to cover the retreat. At 1100 hours the brigade reached the St-Pierre docks basin just south of the citadel mound, and by 1245 hours it was secure along the line of the Orne. A final weak attack at 1500 hours towards St-Pierre by Battlegroup *Rauch*, including two attached companies of II/46th *Luftwaffe* Rifles, was halted by shellfire and pulled back east of the Orne.

On the western side of the town, by midday 8th Canadian Infantry Brigade from Carpiquet village had captured the aerodrome's southern hangars and control tower area that had eluded them on 4 July, pushing a battalion southwards to Bretteville-sur-Odon, and 43rd (Wessex) Division had once more moved troops eastward along the Odon valley into Verson to cover its flank. By 1330 hours 9th Canadian Infantry Brigade had secured Ardennes Abbey and overcome the last resistance at St-Germain-la-Blanche-Herbe. Within the hour, tanks and armoured cars were advancing freely into Caen from the west to link up with 3rd British Infantry Division, and by 1750 hours Caen had been liberated up to the line of the Orne and the Odon. The bridges were destroyed, damaged or blocked with masonry, and the Allied troops made little attempt to cross. The people of Caen started to emerge from their cellars and houses, some into the cratered piles of rubble that had been their streets, and mostly greeted their liberators with genuine relief.

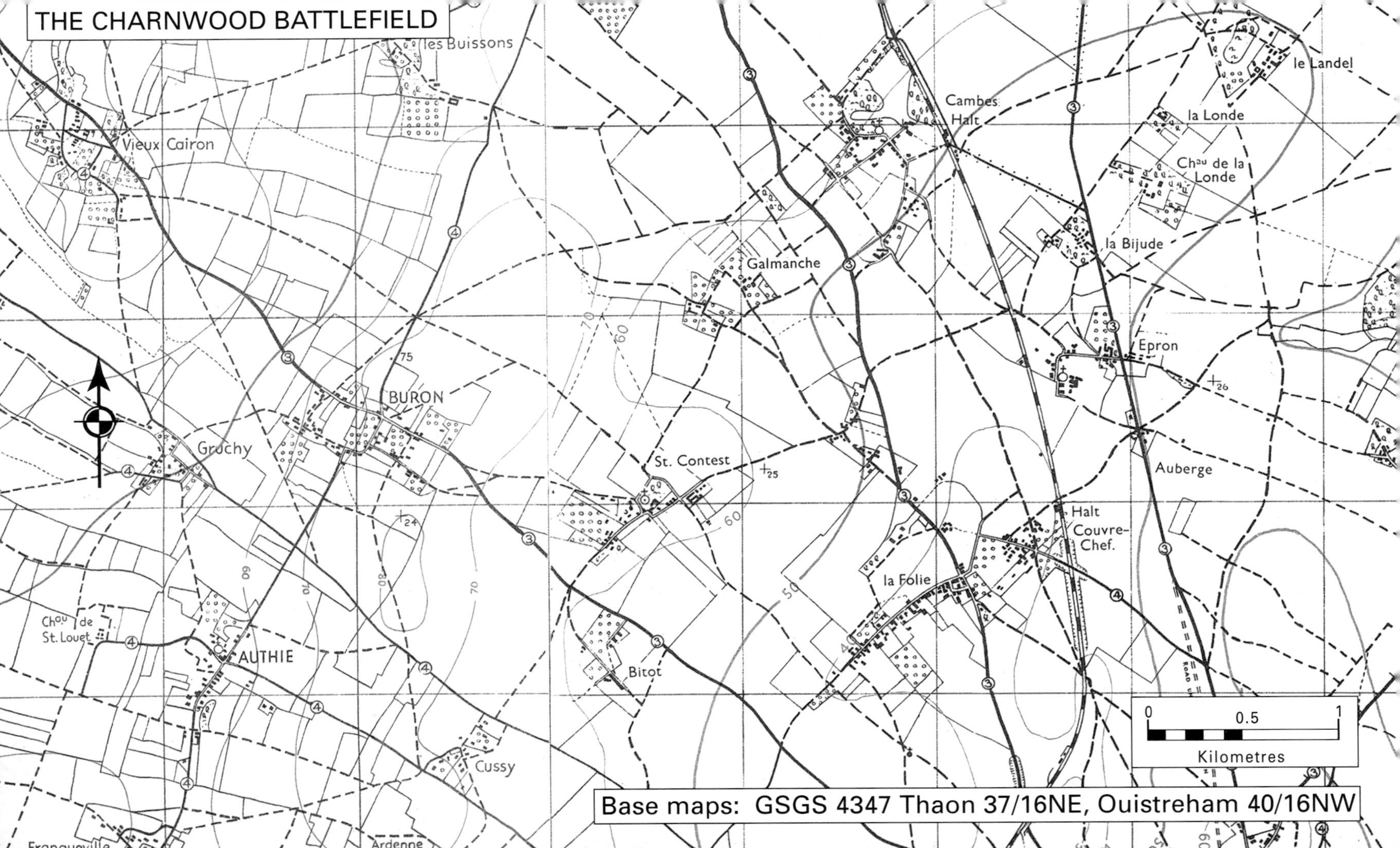
THE CHARNWOOD BATTLEFIELD
les Buissons
Vieux Cairon
Cambes Halt
le Landel
la Londe
Chau de la Londe
la Bijude
Galmanche
Epron
Auberge
BURON
Gruchy
St. Contest
Halt Couvre-Chef.
la Folie
AUTHIE
Chau de St. Louet
Bitot
Cussy
Franqueville
Ardenne
Kilometres
0
0.5
1
Base maps: GSGS 4347 Thaon 37/16NE, Ouistreham 40/16NW

The following night and 10 July were spent mopping up, after which 3rd British Infantry Division moved into I Corps reserve. In the three days of Charnwood, I Corps suffered 3,817 casualties, including 1,194 for 3rd Canadian Division, and lost about 80 tanks. Some battalions recorded the heaviest casualties that they suffered in Normandy: the HLI of Canada lost 262 men, including 62 killed, in taking Buron; 2nd/6th South Staffordshires lost 215 men. Almost 600 Germans were captured, suggesting total losses of over 2,000. 31st *Luftwaffe* Rifles was destroyed, losing its regimental and battalion commanders, and three-quarters of its men. The *Hitlerjugend* Division's incomplete records give losses of 489, including 136 killed and 165 missing. I/25th and II/25th SS Panzergrenadiers lost 85 dead and 205 other casualties between them; losses from III/25th SS Panzergrenadiers are unknown, but the battalion was amalgamated with I/25th SS Panzergrenadiers after the battle. The *Hitlerjugend* also reported losing eleven Panthers and seven Panzer IVs. Losses for other German units are not known.

A Priest self-propelled gun passes a Humber scout car from 30th Armoured Brigade, whose mine-clearing Sherman flail tanks assisted the advance on 8 July. *(IWM B6657)*

No sooner had Charnwood ended than, at 0500 hours on 10 July in the *bocage* to the west of Caen, VIII Corps began Operation 'Jupiter', an attack southwards against II SS Panzer Corps, and by

German infantry retreat through Caen, 9 July. *(BA 495/3427/2)*

next day 43rd Division had captured and consolidated most of Hill 112. This left Panzer Group West uncertain whether the next British 'colossal crack' would come from east or west of Caen. On 13 July VIII Corps headquarters was pulled into reserve for reorganisation, with XII Corps taking over the line west of Caen.

Also on 13 July, British operational research investigators reported that the heavy bombing plan for Operation Charnwood had been misconceived, and that no critical German defences had been destroyed in the bombing. There was a strong suspicion at SHAEF and among the senior airmen that Second Army had misled them about Caen's defences to get Bomber Command to mount the raid. The sight of the bombing had cheered the British and Canadian troops, but the resulting rubble had only slowed their advance into Caen, and French civilians had died for no apparent purpose. For his critics Montgomery could do nothing right, and had not even liberated Caen completely.

The German perspective was very different. On 8 July Hitler ordered Army Group B to give up all attempts at major counter-attacks and to fight a defensive battle until more reinforcements arrived. The German loss of Caen also convinced the French that the Allies could no longer be driven into the sea, and that liberation was becoming a fact. Next day, Field Marshal Rommel told *Oberstleutnant* (Lt-Col) Caesar von Hofacker, one of the conspirators plotting to assassinate Hitler, that the front in Normandy could only hold for another three weeks, and the plan went ahead.

Three relieved-looking residents of Caen greet a group of British soldiers soon after their entry into the city on 9 July. *(IWM B6738)*

CHAPTER 3

OPERATION 'GOODWOOD' – THE PLAN

The fighting for Caen reached its peak after another week, on Tuesday 18 July, with Second Army's launch of Operation 'Goodwood' and its subsidiary Operation 'Atlantic', requiring the heaviest air bombardment and the most powerful concentration of artillery and armour yet assembled by the Allies in Normandy. The attack finally cleared the Germans from Caen and from the ground to the east and south, although at heavy cost to the British and Canadians, which led to even greater argument among the Allies.

On 7 July, before Charnwood started, Montgomery wrote to Field Marshal Sir Alan Brooke, the Chief of the Imperial General Staff in London, that if the operation succeeded by 10 July he was planning 'To get that part of Caen which lies south of the Orne, and to organise operations to just south-east of that axis', while simultaneously pushing south on the west side of the Orne. On 10 July, Montgomery met Lt-Gen Dempsey and Lt Gen Bradley at his headquarters to plan their next attacks. Bradley needed about a week to mount his major break-out attempt in the west, Operation 'Cobra', planned to start on 18 July if St-Lô had been captured. Montgomery's orders to Dempsey were, 'Go on hitting: drawing the German strength, especially the armour, onto yourself – so as to ease the way for Brad.' Second Army was to continue with attacks west of the Orne, but its main tasks were to liberate Faubourg de Vaucelles, and undertake a major offensive using all three British armoured divisions (including the newly arrived Guards Armoured Division, created by converting battalions of foot guards to armour) grouped under Lt-Gen O'Connor's VIII Corps. The arrival of 2nd Canadian Infantry Division made it possible on 11 July to form II Canadian Corps under Lt-Gen Guy Simonds to take part, together with Lt-Gen Crocker's I Corps. However, delays in capturing St-Lô led to Operation Cobra being put back to 20 July, with Second Army's offensive starting two days earlier.

As a preliminary, at 0100 hours on 11 July, 153rd (Highland) Brigade launched a raid east of the Orne against the Colombelles steelworks to destroy two tall chimneys used for observation. At 0500 hours the accompanying Shermans of 148th RAC were ambushed by 13 Tigers of 3/503rd Heavy Panzer Battalion, which destroyed or captured at least nine British tanks without loss, causing the raid to be abandoned and demonstrating clearly the threat posed by Tigers to any future British advance.

The weather was at last improving with more clear skies and sunshine. At 1000 hours on 13 July Lt-Gen Dempsey met his three corps commanders to discuss Second Army's main attack south from the Orne bridgehead, code-named Operation Goodwood, followed later in the day by written orders from Second Army headquarters. On 7 July Eisenhower had written to Montgomery that 'We have not yet attempted a major full dress attack on the left [eastern] flank supported by everything that we could bring to bear. To do so would require good weather, so that our air [power] could give maximum assistance', and on 13 July Montgomery

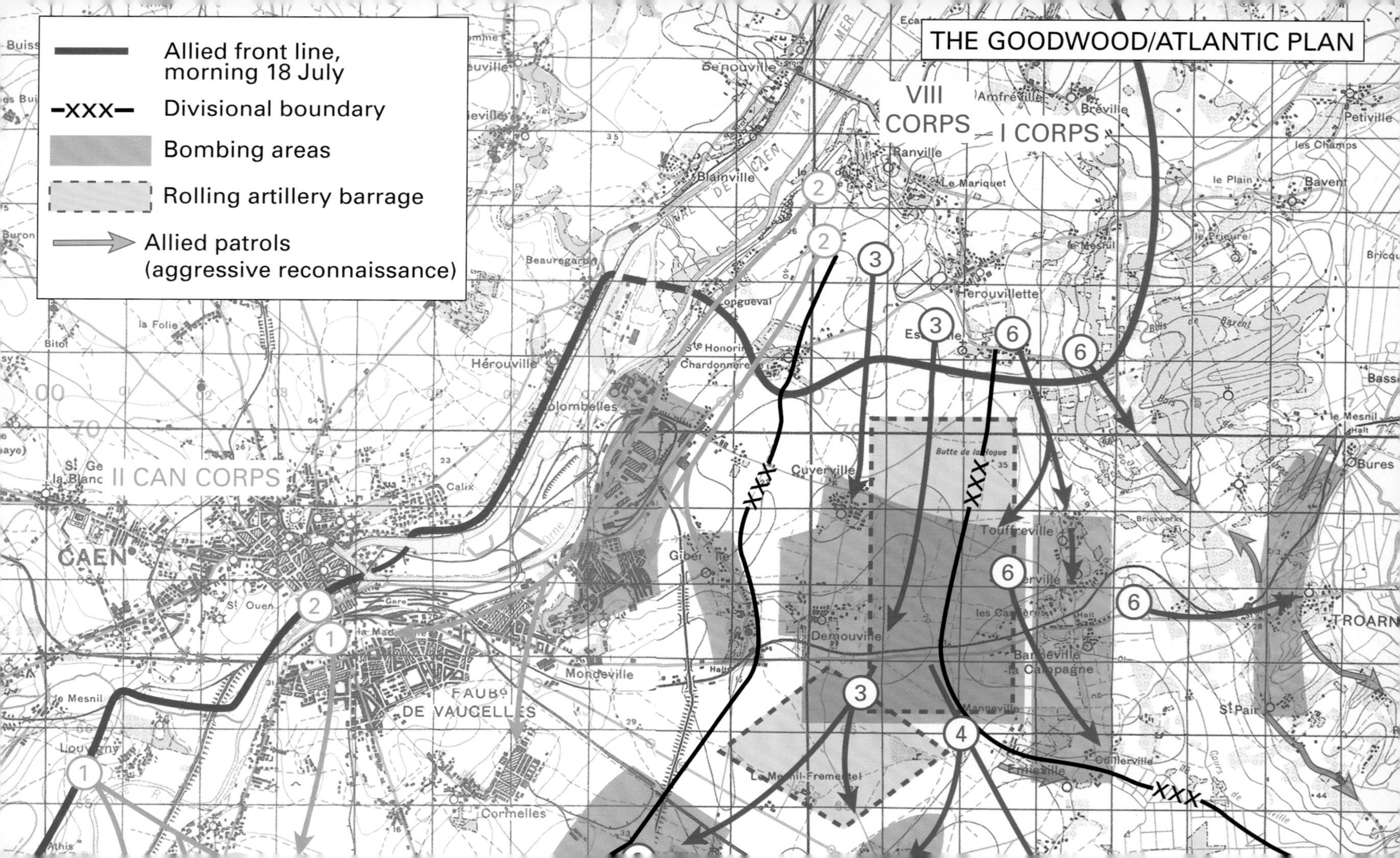
THE GOODWOOD/ATLANTIC PLAN
Allied front line, morning 18 July
Divisional boundary
Bombing areas
Rolling artillery barrage
Allied patrols (aggressive reconnaissance)
VIII CORPS
I CORPS
II CAN CORPS
CAEN
FAUBG DE VAUCELLES
Ranville
Blainville
Amfreville
Bréville
Petiville
Bavent
Hérouvillette
Cuverville
Touffreville
Demouville
Giberville
Colombelles
Mondeville
Cormelles
Troarn
St Pair
Le Mesnil-Frementel
Cuillerville
Emiéville
Banneville la Campagne
Manneville
Hérouville
Longueval
Chardonnerette
Bures
Le Mariquet
les Champs
le Plain
le Prieuré
le Mesnil
St Ouen
Calix
la Folie
Beauregard
Louvigny
les Cagnères
Butte de la Hogue
Brickworks
Bois de Bavent

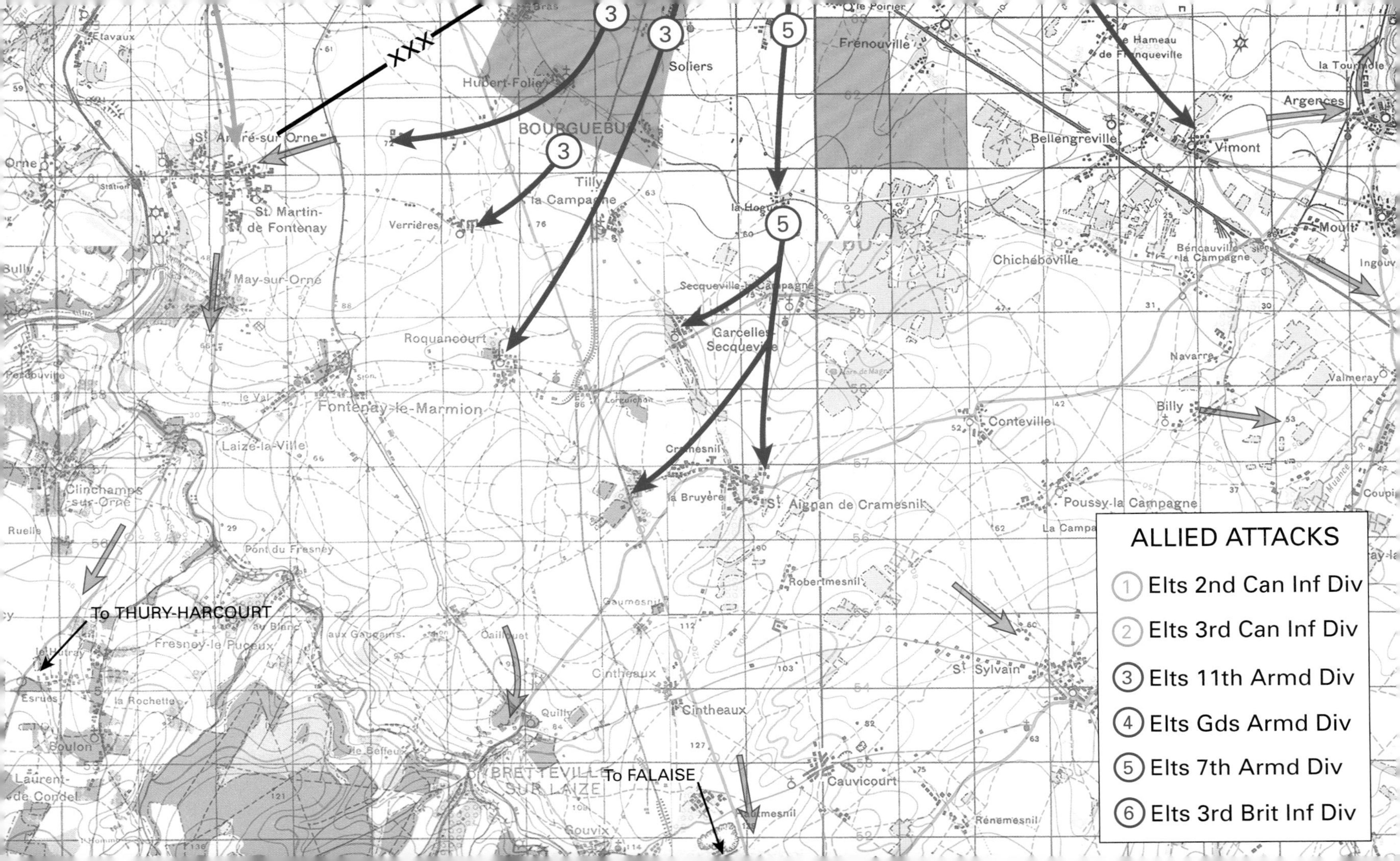
ALLIED ATTACKS
1 Elts 2nd Can Inf Div
2 Elts 3rd Can Inf Div
3 Elts 11th Armd Div
4 Elts Gds Armd Div
5 Elts 7th Armd Div
6 Elts 3rd Brit Inf Div
To THURY-HARCOURT
To FALAISE
XXX
Frénouville
Soliers
Hubert-Folie
Bourguébus
Bellengreville
Vimont
Argences
Moult
Tilly la Campagne
Verrières
St. André-sur-Orne
St. Martin-de Fontenay
May-sur-Orne
Roquancourt
Fontenay-le-Marmion
Secqueville-la-Campagne
Garcelles-Secqueville
Chicheboville
Conteville
Billy
Navarre
Valmeray
Cramesnil
la Bruyère
St. Aignan de Cramesnil
Poussy-la Campagne
Robertmesnil
Gaumesnil
Cintheaux
St. Sylvain
Cauvicourt
Quilly
Bretteville sur Laize
Laize-la-Ville
Clinchamps-sur-Orne
Fresney-le-Puceux
Pont du Fresney
Étavaux
la Hogue
Béneauville la Campagne
Le Hameau de Franqueville
la Tourmole
Rénemesnil
Gouvix
Boulon
la Rochette
Esquay
Laurent-de Condel

replied to Eisenhower on the need for such air power. Next day, Dempsey requested not only Bomber Command but also the Eighth Air Force for bombing on a larger scale even than Charnwood.

Preliminary Second Army operations started after dark on 15 July to the south-west of Caen, as XII Corps attacked, led by 15th (Scottish) and 53rd (Welsh) Divisions, in Operation 'Greenline' to capture high ground south of Évrecy. On 16 July XXX Corps joined in further west with a similar attack led by 59th (Staffordshire) and 49th (West Riding) Divisions towards Noyers in Operation 'Pomegranate'. These battles cost the British 3,500 casualties, but led *General* Eberbach to move the *Hohenstaufen* Division to the west side of the Orne to reinforce the *Frundsberg* Division and 2nd Panzer Division. Dempsey described this as 'tennis across the Orne', forcing the German armoured battlegroups to move from one side of the difficult river valley to the other in response to each threat, and so present targets for the Allied tactical air forces.

For Operation Goodwood, Dempsey planned an advance by VIII Corps from a start line running from Longueval to Escoville villages, held by 51st (Highland) Division, down across the Caen plain and up onto Bourguébus ridge 11 km away, with the chance of getting much further. A set-piece attack in phases was not possible since Second Army lacked the one or more fresh infantry divisions needed to make the first break-through. Instead, Goodwood would depend on massed bombers and artillery blasting through the German battle zone including the village strongpoints, followed by a deep advance by O'Connor's three armoured divisions in succession, together with supporting attacks by I Corps to the east and II Canadian Corps to the west. A four-hour air and artillery bombardment was planned to start at 0525 hours, using high explosive bombs to annihilate German forces in the villages on either side of the main advance by VIII Corps, while artillery shells and fragmentation bombs (to limit cratering) fell on the defenders in the centre, followed by the ground attack starting at 0745 hours. Some 1,300 tanks of all kinds would be used, including 759 Shermans and Cromwells with VIII Corps and 275 with the two flanking corps.

Two significant obstacles cut across the VIII Corps advance over the Caen plain. The first was the railway line running from Caen just south of the villages of Démouville and Sannerville and on to Troarn (the Caen–Troarn or 'first' railway line in many accounts), 4.5 km from the start line with a low 1–2 metre embankment in several places. The second, 2.7 km beyond this, was the double-

The Tiger counter-attack on 11 July (*see p. 49*) led to the capture of several British tanks and anti-tank guns, among them this Sherman Firefly. The Germans used this tank to lead counter-attacks during Operation Goodwood, but it was destroyed on 18 or 19 July. *(BA 496/3455/12)*

tracked railway line running south-easterly from Caen, with alternating embankments and cuttings that presented major obstacles, (the Caen–Vimont or 'second' railway line). This second railway line ran parallel with the N13 main road from Caen to Vimont (and still does), with a small elevation in the centre at the village of Cagny, 6.6 km from the British start line. From the Caen–Vimont railway line to Soliers village was 2 km – lethal 88-mm range – and 3.6 km to Bourguébus village on the north-facing slope of the ridge overlooking the battlefield. The Germans also retained excellent observation from the Colombelles steelworks to the west and from the high ground of Bavent Wood to the east.

Contrary to many later stories, British intelligence had a good picture of Panzer Group West's forces east of the Orne, although any positions beyond the first village barrier had to be confirmed chiefly by air photographs, which were inconclusive. In the front line Second Army expected to find 16th *Luftwaffe* Division, supported by 25th SS Panzergrenadiers (in fact just relieved together with the rest of the *Hitlerjugend* Division, and correctly located in reserve by British signals intelligence before 18 July). Second Army

Allied Order of Battle for Operation Goodwood

Second (British) Army — ***Lt-Gen Sir Miles Dempsey***

4th Army Group Royal Artillery; 8th Army Group Royal Artillery; 2nd Canadian Army Group Royal Artillery

from 79th Armoured Division — ***Maj-Gen Sir Percy Hobart***

22nd Dragoons (Crab flails); 1st Lothians and Border Horse (Crab flails); 141st Regiment, RAC (Churchill Crocodiles), 5th Assault Regiment, Royal Engineers (AVREs)

I Corps — ***Lt-Gen J.T. Crocker***

6th Airborne Division; 1st Special Service Brigade

did not take part in the battle

3rd (British) Infantry Division — ***Maj-Gen L.G. Whistler***

as for Charnwood, *see pp. 40–1*

51st (Highland) Division — ***Maj-Gen D.C. Bullen-Smith***

152nd (Highland) Brigade:
2nd Seaforth Highlanders; 5th Seaforth Highlanders; 5th Queen's Own Cameron Highlanders

153rd (Highland) Brigade:
5th Black Watch; 1st Gordon Highlanders; 5th/7th Gordon Highlanders

154th (Highland) Brigade:
1st Black Watch; 7th Black Watch; 7th Argyll and Sutherland Highlanders

2nd Derbyshire Yeomanry; 1st/7th Middlesex Regt(MG)
126th, 127th and 128th Field Regts, RA; 61st AT Regt, RA; 40th LAA Regt, RA

27th Armoured Brigade

as for Charnwood, *see pp. 40–1*

II Canadian Corps — ***Lt-Gen G.G. Simonds***

2nd Canadian Armoured Brigade

as for Charnwood, *see pp. 40–1*

2nd Canadian Infantry Division — ***Maj-Gen C. Foulkes***

4th Canadian Infantry Brigade:
Royal Regt of Canada; Royal Hamilton Light Infantry; Essex Scottish Regt

5th Canadian Infantry Brigade:
Black Watch of Canada; Le Régiment de Maisonneuve; Calgary Highlanders

6th Canadian Infantry Brigade:
Les Fusiliers Mont-Royal; Queen's Own Cameron Highlanders of Canada; South Saskatchewan Regt

14th Canadian Hussars (8th Recce Regt); Toronto Scottish Regt (MG)
4th, 5th, 6th Field Regts, RCA; 2nd AT Regt, RCA; 3rd LAA Regt, RCA

3rd Canadian Division — ***Maj-Gen R.F.L. Keller***

as for Charnwood, *see pp. 40–1*

VIII Corps *Lt-Gen Sir Richard O'Connor*

Guards Armoured Division *Maj-Gen A.H.S. Adair*

5th Guards Armoured Brigade:
2nd (Armd) Grenadier Guards; 1st (Armd) Coldstream Guards; 2nd (Armd) Irish Guards; 1st (Motor) Grenadier Guards

32nd Guards Brigade:
5th Coldstream Guards; 3rd Irish Guards; 1st Welsh Guards

2nd (Armd Recce) Welsh Guards
55th and 153rd Field Regts, RA; 21st AT Regt, RA; 94th LAA Regt, RA

7th Armoured Division *Maj-Gen G.W.E.J. Erskine*

22nd Armoured Brigade:
4th County of London Yeomanry (Sharpshooters); 1st Royal Tank Regt, 5th Royal Tank Regt; 1st (Motor) Battalion, Rifle Brigade

131st Infantry Brigade:
1st/5th Queen's Regt; 1st/6th Queen's Regt; 1st/7th Queen's Regt

8th Kings Royal Irish Hussars
3rd and 5th Regts, RHA; 65th AT Regt, RA; 15th LAA Regt, RA

11th Armoured Division *Maj-Gen G.P.B. Roberts*

29th Armoured Brigade:
23rd Hussars; 2nd Fife & Forfar Yeomanry; 3rd Royal Tank Regt; 8th (Motor) Battalion, Rifle Brigade

159th Infantry Brigade:
3rd Monmouthshire Regt; 4th King's Shropshire Light Infantry; 1st Herefordshire Regt

2nd Northamptonshire Yeomanry
13th Regt, RHA; 151st Field Regt, RA; 75th AT Regt, RA; 58th LAA Regt, RA

Attached
The Inns of Court Regiment (Reconnaissance)

Two days before Goodwood begins, a cheerful-looking Montgomery, Dempsey and O'Connor meet to finalise plans. *(IWM B7407)*

expected battlegroups of 21st Panzer Division about 8 km back along the line of the N13 road near Vimont, Cagny, and Vaucelles with about 50 Panzer IVs and 35 assault guns; and the *Leibstandarte* Division in reserve with 40 Panthers and 60 Panzer IVs (the correct figure was 46 Panthers and 61 Panzer IVs). It also expected to fight two Tiger battalions, but wrongly placed both with I SS Panzer Corps; 503rd Heavy Panzer Battalion had been recently attached to 21st Panzer Division in LXXXVI Corps, and was unidentified. This apparently small error in the intelligence picture would make a big difference in the battle. German artillery east of the Orne was assessed as 300 field and anti-tank guns (close to Rommel's own description of 194 field guns and 90 anti-tank guns), including 90 pieces in the centre of the battle zone and another 40 on its flanks, then weak defences and only about 20 guns up to the Caen–Vimont railway line. Second Army and VIII Corps also identified a second powerful line of guns along the north slopes of the Bourguébus ridge, but were unsure of its exact strength and location.

German troops on the Bois de Bavent ridgeline had superb views over the Goodwood battlefield. This photo was taken from 1 km north of Touffréville, and shows the open plain crossed by VIII Corps on 18 July. The distant avenue of trees on the left runs along the D226 Cuverville–Sannerville road. *(SCT)*

This was a very accurate estimate. I SS Panzer Corps headquarters was at Urville, 15km south of Caen just off the Falaise road, with 101st Heavy SS Panzer Battalion (no more than six operational Tigers on 18 July) nearby. I SS Panzer Corps reserve also included a few heavy guns of 101st SS Artillery Battalion and *Nebelwerfers* of 7th Werfer Brigade. On 14 July II/980th Grenadiers and I/980th Grenadiers of the newly arrived 272nd Infantry Division took over the defence of Vaucelles from the *Leibstandarte* Division, which pulled back into local reserve between the village of Ifs and the east bank of the Orne, sending a strong battlegroup (II/1st SS Panzers, III/1st SS Panzergrenadiers, 1st SS Assault Gun Battalion and I/1st SS Panzer Artillery) west of the Orne as I SS Panzer Corps reserve.

A British 5.5-inch gun opens fire during the offensive in the Odon valley, 16 July. *(IWM B7413)*

Next day, the badly weakened *Hitlerjugend* Division was put into OKW reserve to refit. Its divisional artillery regiment and anti-aircraft artillery battalion were left to support 272nd Infantry Division, and some units were pulled out of the division altogether. The weak Battlegroup *Waldmüller*, including II/12th SS Panzers (five Panthers and three Panzer IVs) and the amalgamated 25th SS Panzergrenadiers, moved southwards to rest 8 km north of Falaise, and the stronger Battlegroup *Wünsche* consisting of I/12th SS Panzers (13 Panthers and 18 Panzer IVs), I/26th and III/26th SS Panzergrenadiers and a light motorised battery of I/12th SS Panzer Artillery moved 40 km east of Caen to Lisieux. It was critically important to Montgomery that none of this German armour should be sent across to oppose Bradley's forthcoming Cobra offensive.

King Tigers of 1/503rd Heavy Tank Battalion hide from Allied aerial reconnaissance. The photo was taken just before Operation Goodwood, near Argences. *(BA 721/359/37)*

On 15 July German military intelligence warned that a British attack east of the Orne was likely from 17 July onwards, but towards the south-east and Paris rather than directly south. Through their code-breakers, the British were aware of these German expectations. On 17 July *General* Eberbach halted the move of Battlegroup *Waldmüller* eastward to join the rest of the *Hitlerjugend* Division at Lisieux. In LXXXVI Corps' sector, defending the Orne bridgehead, the front was held, as the British knew, by 16th *Luftwaffe* Field Division, now quite weak. I/32nd *Luftwaffe* Rifles with its flank on the Orne just north of Colombelles faced 3rd Canadian Division, then in the centre II/32nd *Luftwaffe* Rifles and I/46th *Luftwaffe* Rifles faced 11th Armoured Division leading VIII Corps, with II/46th *Luftwaffe* Rifles, 1/16th *Luftwaffe* Artillery and at least one battery of 1053rd Anti-Tank Battalion (75-mm guns) in support. To the east, 3rd British Infantry Division faced 346th Infantry Division, also a weak division that had suffered frequent desertions, largely from Poles and Russians in its ranks. In the immediate path of 3rd British Infantry Division's attack were 857th Grenadiers defending the area of Touffréville, with 858th Grenadiers further to the south, each deployed with two battalions forward and one in reserve, supported

by 346th Assault Gun Company. The rest of 346th Infantry Division extended northwards towards the sea facing British 6th Airborne Division, which had only a supporting role in the battle.

LXXXVI Corps was heavily reinforced with additional artillery to the east and south-east, including 555th Artillery Battalion and 1151st Artillery Battalion, each with twelve 122-mm Russian howitzers, 763rd Artillery Battalion with 170-mm guns, 1193rd Artillery Battalion with 149-mm guns (of Italian origin), and the mobile heavy guns of 725th Railway Artillery. The corps rear zone, never voluntarily given up in German tactics, ran from just in front of Troarn south to Vimont and then west across Bourguébus ridge.

German Order of Battle for Operation Goodwood

Panzer Group West *(Panzergruppe West)*
General der Panzertruppen Heinrich Eberbach

I SS Panzer Corps
SS-Obergruppenführer Josef Dietrich

1st SS Panzer Division *(1. SS-Panzerdivision 'Leibstandarte Adolf Hitler')*
SS-Obergruppenführer Theodore Wisch

1st SS Panzer Regiment; 1st & 2nd SS Panzergrenadier Regts;
1st SS Artillery Regiment; 1st SS Reconnaissance Battalion;
(plus support units)

12th SS Panzer Division *(12. SS-Panzerdivision 'Hitlerjugend')*
SS-Brigadeführer Kurt Meyer

12th SS Panzer Regiment; 25th & 26th SS Panzergrenadier Regts;
12th SS Artillery Regiment; 12th SS Reconnaissance Battalion;
(plus support units)

272nd Infantry Division *(272. Infanteriedivision)*
Generalleutnant Friedrich Schack

980th, 981st, 982nd Infantry Regiments;
272nd Artillery Regt; 272nd Reconnaissance Btn; 272nd Anti-Tank Btn

101st SS Heavy Panzer Battalion *(schwere SS-Panzer Abteilung 101.)*

101st SS Artillery Battalion *(SS-Artillerieabteilung 101.)*

7th Werfer Brigade *(Werferbrigade 7.)*

83rd Werfer Regiment; 84th Werfer Regiment

LXXXVI Corps
General der Infanterie Hans von Obstfelder

21st Panzer Division *(21. Panzerdivision)*
Generalmajor Edgar Feuchtinger

22nd Panzer Regiment; 125th & 192nd Panzergrenadier Regiments;
155th Artillery Regt; 21st Reconnaissance Btn; 200th Assault Gun Btn;
(plus support units)

503rd Heavy Panzer Battalion *(schwere Panzer Abteilung 503)*

16th Luftwaffe Field Division *(16. Luftwaffenfelddivision)*
Generalleutnant Karl Sievers

31st, 32nd, 46th Luftwaffe Rifle Regiments;
16th Luftwaffe Artillery Regiment; 16th Luftwaffe Anti-Tank Battalion

In reserve behind 16th *Luftwaffe* Division in LXXXVI Corps centre was 21st Panzer Division. After Charnwood, 22nd Panzers was also left very weak, with about 50 Panzer IVs altogether on 17 July, but the division was strengthened by 200th Assault Gun Battalion (*Sturmgeschütz Abteilung 200*), an improvised formation of self-propelled 75-mm anti-tank guns and 105-mm howitzers on

346th Infantry Division *(346. Infanteriedivision)*
Generalleutnant Erich Straube
857th & 858th Infantry Regiments;
346th Artillery Regt; 346th Reconnaissance Btn; 346th Anti-Tank Btn

711th Infantry Division *(711. Infanteriedivision)*
Generalleutnant Josef Reichert
731st & 744th Infantry Regiments;
1711th Artillery Regiment; 711th Anti-Tank Company

9th Werfer Brigade *(Werferbrigade 9)*
14th & 54th Werfer Regiments

Other Artillery Units
555th, 763rd, 1151st & 1193rd Artillery Battalions
(Heeres Artillerie Abteilungen)
1255th Heavy Coastal Artillery Battalion
(schwere Heeres Küsten Artillerie Abteilung)
1039th & 1053rd Anti-Tank Battalions *(Heeres Artillerie Pak Abteilungen)*
725th Railway Artillery Battalion *(Eisenbahn Artillerie Abteilung 725)*

21st Panzer Division's combat power was enhanced by vehicles like this one, mounting a 75-mm anti-tank gun on a French tank chassis. Four of these self-propelled guns were operated by each of the first four batteries of the division's 200th Assault Gun Battalion. *(BA 493/3365/20)*

French tank chassis, and by some towed 88-mm Pak 43/41 guns with its anti-tank battalion. 22nd Panzers was also supported by 503rd Heavy Panzer Battalion with 27 Tigers and 12 even more powerful Tiger II 'King Tigers' (*Königstiger* – not yet encountered in battle by the British), in its 1st Company. The western half of the battlefield behind 16th *Luftwaffe* Field Division, including the

Colombelles steelworks area, was defended by I/192nd Panzergrenadiers, with II/192nd Panzergrenadiers further south in the area of Soliers, Hubert-Folie and Bras (the modern Ifs Bras). The eastern half was defended by 125th Panzergrenadiers under *Major* Hans von Luck as the core of Battlegroup *von Luck*, which included additional artillery and the self-propelled guns of 200th Assault Gun Battalion. In a convoluted command arrangement, I/192nd Panzergrenadiers came under 16th *Luftwaffe* Division, while II/46th *Luftwaffe* Rifles came under 21st Panzer Division.

View from the western edge of Sannerville, looking north past Touffréville church (*left centre*) to the dense woodland beyond, which was the scene of heavy fighting between 152nd (Highland) Brigade and German troops on 18 July. *(SCT)*

The Panzergrenadiers, together with the towed anti-tank guns and assault guns, dug themselves into the villages of the Caen plain. 1/200th Assault Gun Battalion was located at Démouville with elements of I/125th Panzergrenadiers; 2/200th was at Giberville with 10 Panzer IVs of 22nd Panzer and two companies of I/192nd Panzergrenadiers; 3/200th was at Grentheville with more 75-mm anti-tank guns from 1053rd Anti-Tank Battalion, at least 24 *Nebelwerfers* from 14th Werfer Regiment (plus roughly as many in the fields to the east), and about one company of 125th Panzergrenadiers; 4/200th was near le Mesnil Frémentel farm and hamlet with the headquarters of I/125th Panzergrenadiers; and 5/200th was part of the garrison at nearby le Prieuré farm.

The position of 21st Panzer Division's armour in reserve (other than the detachment at Giberville) conformed to standard German tactics. But on 15 July Rommel ordered 22nd Panzers moved further forward and to the east to defend against a south-easterly Allied attack, a change also identified by British signals intelligence. I/22nd Panzers was deployed near Sannerville with some *Nebelwerfers* of 54th Werfer Regiment, 3rd Company (Flak) 16th *Luftwaffe* Assault Gun Battalion, and a reinforced company of II/125th Panzer-grenadiers; II/22nd Panzers was deployed with the King Tigers of 1/503rd Heavy Panzer Battalion between Émiéville and Guillerville farm ('Cuillerville' on British maps), with 2/503rd Heavy Panzer Battalion 2 km further east. The headquarters of both 22nd Panzers and 503rd Heavy Panzer Battalion were at Émiéville together with four 122-mm guns of 1/155th Panzer Artillery; 3/503rd Heavy Panzer Battalion was nearby in the wooded grounds of Manneville stud. This left 220th Panzer Engineer Battalion and part of II/192nd Panzergrenadiers at Soliers and Bourguébus as the divisional reserve. *Major* von Luck's headquarters and that of 155th Panzer Artillery were at Frénouville, and 21st Panzer Division headquarters was back behind the ridge at Conteville.

The Germans deployed a number of 88-mm flak guns among their defences near the Bourguébus Ridge. This example was photographed beside the Caen–Vimont railway. *(Tank Museum, Bovington)*

The German gun line defending Bourguébus ridge was a mix of anti-tank, field and medium guns and *Nebelwerfers*. There were some 88-mm Flak guns in the area from 2nd Anti-Aircraft Assault Regiment (*Flak-Sturm Regiment 2*) of III Flak Corps: one battery of four guns was in Cagny, and probably another two batteries close to Bourguébus village; but most of this *Luftwaffe* formation was well behind the ridge, defending the Caen–Falaise road against Allied aircraft. The 75-mm Pak guns of 1053rd Anti-Tank Battalion defending Grentheville may have been joined by a battery of 88-mm Flak guns to the west near Cormelles. Some of 1053rd Anti-Tank Battalion faced north-west in front of Frénouville, covering the gap between Cagny and Émiéville. The main gun line along the ridge was on the north-facing slope in the centre, covering the approach between Grentheville and Cagny. Two batteries of 305th Flak Battalion from 21st Panzer Division with eight – at least – 88-mm guns were deployed on either side of la Hogue, with 18 field guns of 16th *Luftwaffe* Artillery downslope in front of them and more guns further downslope between Frénouville and Soliers, including II/ and III/155th Panzer Artillery (105-mm and 155-mm guns) and 18 guns (either 122-mm or 155-mm) of 1255th Coastal Artillery, relocated from their original positions on D-Day. To the west, 2/155th Panzer Artillery, with four 122-mm guns, formed part of the defence of Bras and Hubert-Folie, together with some 88-mm guns of 200th Panzer Anti-Tank Battalion. This meant about 36 anti-tank guns spread across the German rear position including probably no more than 8–16 on Bourguébus ridge itself, together with 48 field and medium guns and about as many *Nebelwerfers*.

On 13 July Second Army issued its first orders for Operation Goodwood. On the eastern flank 3rd British Infantry Division with 152nd (Highland) Brigade was to capture the area from Touffréville to Émiéville including Troarn, a region of particularly dense and often swampy *bocage*. On the western flank II Canadian Corps chose its own code-name, Operation Atlantic, issuing orders on 16 July. For this attack two brigades of 3rd Canadian Infantry Division would clear the east bank of the Orne from Colombelles all the way southwards, including the village of Giberville, to establish bridges over the Orne at Vaucelles. The third brigade would also cross the Orne from southern Caen, and liberate Vaucelles directly, followed by 2nd Canadian Infantry Division which would push south along both banks of the river. The orders for Lt-Gen O'Connor's central punch through the German line were for 11th Armoured Division to drive down the Caen plain and south-west over the Bourguébus ridge, aiming for Bretteville-sur-Laize west of the Caen–Falaise road; next the Guards Armoured Division's objectives were Vimont and Argences to the south-east on the N13;

and 7th Armoured Division following up was to aim due south for Falaise itself, more than 30 km away. Next day, Montgomery wrote to Field Marshal Brooke that, before Second Army declined in strength, 'I have decided to have a real show-down on the east flank, and to loose a Corps of three armoured divisions into the open country about the Caen– Falaise road.' On 16 July SHAEF agreed to the heavy bombers providing support for Operation Goodwood on the basis of Second Army's 13 July order; Eisenhower described himself as 'so pepped up' about the plan. Tactical air support came from both 83 Group (with some units of 84 Group already under its command) and Ninth Air Force. A Forward Air Control Post, consisting of an RAF officer and his Army assistant in a Sherman or a Stuart light tank able to talk directly to the pilots overhead, was attached to each brigade headquarters of VIII Corps.

Hawker Typhoon fighter-bombers like these, taxiing on a Normandy airfield, played an important role during Goodwood by helping to repel German armoured counter-attacks. *(IWM CL403)*

The mentions of distant Falaise, like the mention of Caen on D-Day, were the source of much angry controversy after the battle. When asked seven years later, Lt-Gen Dempsey denied ever knowing about the 13 July order issued in his name, and maintained that Montgomery had turned down his own suggestion for a deep break-out. But Dempsey also wanted his troops to have positive objectives, and more than one tank crew remembered their orders as 'Head for Falaise; don't stop for anything'; 2nd (Armoured) Irish Guards were told that everyone 'from the Prime Minister downwards' set great store on a big victory.

On 15 July Montgomery took the unusual step of issuing Dempsey with a special written directive on Goodwood, with a copy to O'Connor. This gave his intentions as to engage the German armour and 'write it down' (a characteristic and highly ambiguous Montgomery phrase), and to improve the eastern bridgehead over the Orne. The role of O'Connor's armoured divisions was now 'to dominate the area Bourguébus–Vimont–Bretteville' or the length of the Bourguébus ridge, 'but armoured cars should push far to the south towards Falaise', and once the Canadians had cleared the open ground south of Vaucelles, 'then VIII Corps can "crack about" as the situation demands'. On 17 July, Dempsey gave a further written order to his corps commanders, confirming the objectives south-west for 11th Armoured Division and south-east for Guards Armoured Division, but limiting 7th Armoured Division's advance southwards to the far side of the ridge beyond Garcelles-Secqueville, adding that the divisions must not advance further without his own orders. On 18 July Dempsey stayed with his own tactical headquarters close to O'Connor's in case the German front collapsed completely by midday, in which case he would have ordered a deeper advance. These new orders, never seen by Eisenhower or SHAEF, significantly changed the nature of Goodwood from a deep break-out to a limited attack. Dempsey later admitted that, to get the heavy bombers he needed, Montgomery would have probably over-sold the Goodwood plan to SHAEF, and with staff officers, messages and rumours criss-crossing the Channel, there was a strong air of plot as well as urgency about the planning of Goodwood.

There was no room for VIII Corps together with I Corps in the constricted Orne bridgehead before the battle started, and barely room for one armoured division at a time. Instead, VIII Corps formed up in reserve on the open ground west of the Canal de Caen. After dark on 16 July, Maj-Gen 'Pip' Roberts, commanding 11th Armoured Division (at 37 the youngest divisional commander in the British Army), moved his headquarters and 159th Infantry Brigade in its lorries eastwards across into the Orne bridgehead. Other forces followed next night, including 8th Canadian Infantry Brigade. Given the lack of space in Second Army area, trying to move more than 8,000 vehicles for VIII Corps and its supports without the Germans noticing was very difficult. The only bridges

'York' Bridge, seen on 18 July with a Cromwell tank of 7th Armoured Division crossing into the Orne bridgehead beyond. *(IWM)*

across the canal and the Orne north of Caen had been captured on D-Day by 6th Airborne Division, and named Pegasus Bridge and Horsa Bridge. These two bridges were code-named 'Euston' bridge, leading to two separate routes for tracked and wheeled vehicles both code-named 'Holly' and marked out southwards to the start line. A temporary Bailey bridge was built 300 metres to the south as 'London' bridge leading to the 'Briar' routes, and another 1,000 metres to the north as 'York' bridge leading to the 'Palm' routes. Moving the armoured and lorried infantry brigades of the three divisions in sequence across these bridges (plus 9th Canadian Infantry Brigade, crossing after 11th Armoured Division) and southwards to the start line needed the strictest traffic control.

Three weeks before, 51st (Highland) Division, responsible for marking the final stage of the approach routes, had laid a minefield in front of its positions between Ste-Honorine la Chardronette and Escoville. The mines had been disturbed by shelling and hidden by growing crops, and an attempt to clear them all after dark on 15 July was unsuccessful. Instead, I Corps ordered paths each 40 feet

Cromwell tanks and other Guards Armoured Division vehicles in their assembly area, 18 July. *(IWM B7651)*

(13 metres) wide cleared through the minefield for the advance. By morning on 18 July, at least 19 gaps had been cleared across the front, wired off with cattle fences, and marked with white tape. After the battle Lt-Gen O'Connor sent Lt-Gen Crocker a formal letter thanking the Highland Division for this difficult and dangerous task; but even so the British armoured divisions experienced problems and some losses in these minefields on 18 July.

On the evening of 17 July the medium and heavy guns of 8th AGRA supporting VIII Corps took up positions north-west of Caen between Authie and St-Contest. Together with 4th AGRA supporting I Corps, this artillery had the task of engaging German guns as far as the second railway line. II Canadian Corps was supported by its own 2nd Canadian AGRA, and even by XII Corps' artillery from west of the Orne. German heavy batteries beyond the range of Second Army's artillery, including those further east along the coast, would be attacked from the air, and by HMS *Roberts* and the cruisers HMS *Mauritius* (twelve 6-inch guns) and HMS *Enterprise* (seven 6-inch guns).

Including divisional artillery, Operation Goodwood was supported by 760 guns; the same number as the brigade-sized Operation Windsor, and for the same purpose. The advance of 11th Armoured Division in the centre was to be led by a rolling barrage by eight field regiments with 196 towed or self-propelled 25-pounder field guns. During this barrage, the division's Sexton (self-propelled 25-pounder) regiment would join in the advance. Bourguébus ridge was at the extreme range for the medium artillery, and once the first stage of the battle was over it was planned to move three medium regiments with 5.5-inch guns south to Cagny. Meanwhile the Eighth Air Force would bomb the German gun positions from the second railway line to the ridge, the last bombs falling at 0930 hours.

Neither Lt-Gen O'Connor commanding VIII Corps nor Maj-Gen Roberts commanding 11th Armoured Division was happy with the Goodwood plan. The corridor for VIII Corps' advance up to the Caen–Troarn railway line lay between Cuverville and Démouville to the west, and Touffréville and Sannerville to the east, a gap barely 2 km wide in an area so flat and open it had been a drop zone for British paratroopers on D-Day. The two eastern villages were objectives for 3rd British Infantry Division, but VIII Corps' orders of 16 July required Roberts to capture Cuverville and Démouville, which would take his entire 159th Infantry Brigade with supporting artillery, leaving his 29th Armoured Brigade to advance one Sherman battalion at a time 100 metres behind the rolling barrage southwards for 4.3 km past the Caen–Troarn railway line. The tanks were expected to reach this objective by 0830 hours and then to spread out to a two-battalion front, following the barrage as it switched to a south-westerly axis for a further 2 km to le Mesnil Frémentel farm, the last shell being fired at 0905 hours. This was not a mad tank charge (or 'death ride' as it was later fancifully described), but a controlled tactical advance at 150 metres a minute (8 km/hr or 5 mph), that was expected to reach the Caen–Vimont railway line by 0940 hours. In fact, 29th Armoured Brigade had orders not to advance onto Bourguébus ridge until Eighth Air Force's bombing had stopped at 0930 hours. The brigade was then to press up onto the ridge, swinging south-westward to secure Bras, Hubert-Folie, Verrières and the Caen–Falaise road.

This would commit about 190 British tanks against the heavy German gun concentration on the ridge. But Roberts' immediate problem was Cagny, which was to receive 650 tons of bombs but was still likely to be defended, and which he had no way of taking without more infantry. The solution offered was for 29th Armoured Brigade to 'mask' Cagny, leaving some armour west of the village as a protection against any counter-attack until the Guards Armoured Division came up to capture it. According to Roberts, he was told that, if he still had doubts, another division could lead the attack: senior officers' code for 'shut up and obey orders'.

Suggestions were made that Second Army should plan a more limited attack to capture only the German battle positions and the first railway line, but Montgomery needed a much bigger success for many reasons. With the issue of Caen hanging over him, he was even in trouble with Prime Minister Winston Churchill; on 17 July Montgomery had asked Eisenhower for no visitors for a few days because of the need to preserve secrecy, next day Eisenhower told Churchill, and Churchill flew into a towering rage believing that Montgomery had tried to give him orders.

There was also one piece of news which Montgomery would only discover later. At 1830 hours on 17 July Field Marshal Rommel's staff car was hit by cannon fire from a passing Spitfire and Rommel was badly injured in the resulting crash. For the next day's battle Army Group B had no commander, and fought only according to its training and existing plans.

CHAPTER 4

OPERATION 'GOODWOOD' – THE BATTLE

The combined Operation Goodwood/Operation Atlantic offensive on Tuesday 18 July fell into two succeeding and overlapping attacks. The first of these was the general onslaught by all three corps as far south as the Caen–Troarn railway line. The second was the drive onwards by VIII Corps to the N13 road and the Caen–Vimont railway line, and the attempts to continue onto the Bourguébus ridge, while the flanking corps fought their own battles.

By 0110 hours on 18 July, 3rd British Infantry Division and the rest of I Corps were ready; 8th and 9th Canadian Infantry Brigades were moving into position for Operation Atlantic; and the rest of 11th Armoured Division including 29th Armoured Brigade had crossed the Orne during the night and was moving forward to its start line, with the Guards Armoured Division and 7th Armoured Division waiting 5,000 metres west of their designated bridges. Although the Germans expected to be attacked, and despite the Orne bridgehead being overlooked, Second Army had achieved a considerable degree of surprise.

Despite weighing almost 60 tons, this Tiger I was flipped over with ease by the aerial bombardment that preceded Operation Goodwood. Astonishingly, three of the crew survived, and despite being burned by leaking battery acid were eventually rescued from the tank. *(IWM B8032)*

At dawn the skies were clear with some white clouds, and at the height of summer this would be a hot, long and very dusty day. Second Army started with counter-battery fire against German anti-aircraft positions at 0525 hours; then the first of 1,056 Lancasters and Halifaxes of Bomber Command flew over, once more in their loose 'gaggle' formation at just over 3,000 feet led by 8 (Pathfinder) Group. At 0545 hours, in the half-light of dawn, the Pathfinder aircraft released their flares and 4,800 tons of high explosive bombs came down equally on Colombelles and its steelworks, on Cagny, and deliberately onto 21st Panzer Division's tanks between

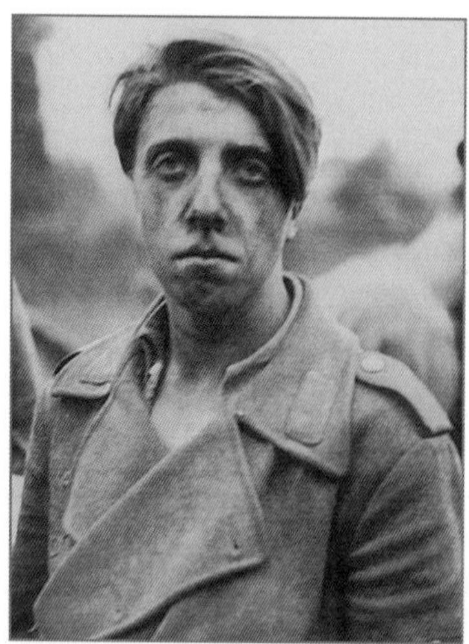

The bombardment's effects are well illustrated by this photo, which shows a traumatised survivor of 200th Assault Gun Battalion. This picture was originally captioned as 'a brutal degenerate looking type of Nazi'. *(IWM B7666)*

Touffréville and Émiéville. Under the explosions men literally went mad or shot themselves; others were blown to fragments or left dazed and incoherent. About half of Cagny was obliterated. Both 503rd Heavy Panzer Battalion and 22nd Panzer Regiment were temporarily put out of action. Some tanks were damaged, others were tossed into the air and overturned by the exploding bombs; after the battle the British counted 20 abandoned tanks in the bomb craters. It would be hours before others could be repaired and re-manned. Only six bombers were shot down by German flak.

At 0640 hours the full Second Army artillery fire-plan began, and for three more hours bombs and shells crashed down on the German defenders, with devastating effects. Twenty minutes later 318 B-26 Marauder bombers of Ninth Air Force, flying in box formation at 10,000–13,000 feet just below the cloudbase, attacked the villages defended by 16th *Luftwaffe* Division with 563 tons of fragmentation bombs. Most were reduced to rubble: at Démouville, 1/200th Assault Gun Battalion was almost destroyed; and 2/200th at Giberville was damaged. Finally, 570 B-24 Liberators of Eighth Air Force's 2nd and 3rd Bombardment Divisions, flying in tight box formation just above 7,500 feet to be clear of medium flak, dropped 1,340 tons of fragmentation bombs on the Troarn area, and onto the main gun line between Bourguébus and Frénouville. Some guns were destroyed outright, others were left damaged or without crews; the *Nebelwerfers* in the open were particularly vulnerable. But in the dust, haze and smoke some aircraft did not bomb through failure to identify targets, and as bombs fell all over the area a few villages were missed, in particular Touffréville in the east and Grentheville in the south. Backing up the bombers were ten wings of the RAF's 83 and 84 Groups and ten fighter-bomber groups (equivalent to RAF wings) of Ninth Air Force: more than 800 aircraft.

Infantry pose for the cameramen on a Sherman tank near Ranville on the morning of 18 July. A Firefly and a Crab flail tank (used for clearing minefields, though no German ones were encountered that day) are visible in the background. *(IWM B7510)*

At 0745 hours, on schedule, the 25-pounder guns supporting 11th Armoured Division started their rolling barrage. 3rd Royal Tank Regiment (3rd RTR), leading 29th Armoured Brigade, advanced south with its accompanying troops and vehicles including a company in half-tracks of 8th Rifle Brigade (an infantry battalion despite its title, actually of the London Rifle Brigade), followed by a similar battalion group led by 2nd Fife and Forfar Yeomanry and a third group led by 23rd Hussars. Simultaneously, two more field regiments, six medium regiments and all three heavy regiments shelled Cuverville, Démouville and Giberville. 159th Infantry Brigade moved off on foot, supported by the Cromwell tanks of 2nd Northamptonshire Yeomanry, to tackle the defenders of Cuverville and a nearby orchard, and then Démouville, while armoured cars of the Inns of Court Regiment followed 29th Armoured Brigade to investigate the situation further south. After the bombing and shelling the *Luftwaffe* troops were in no condition

THE GOODWOOD BATTLEFIELD
Hérouvillette
River Orne
Orne R.
Colombelles
Ste. Honorine
la Chardonerette
Escoville
Pre. Baron
Butte de la Hogue
Cuverville
Touffreville
Giberville
Demouville
Sannerville
Lirose
Halt
Mondeville
Bellemaist
FAUBg. DE VAUCELLES

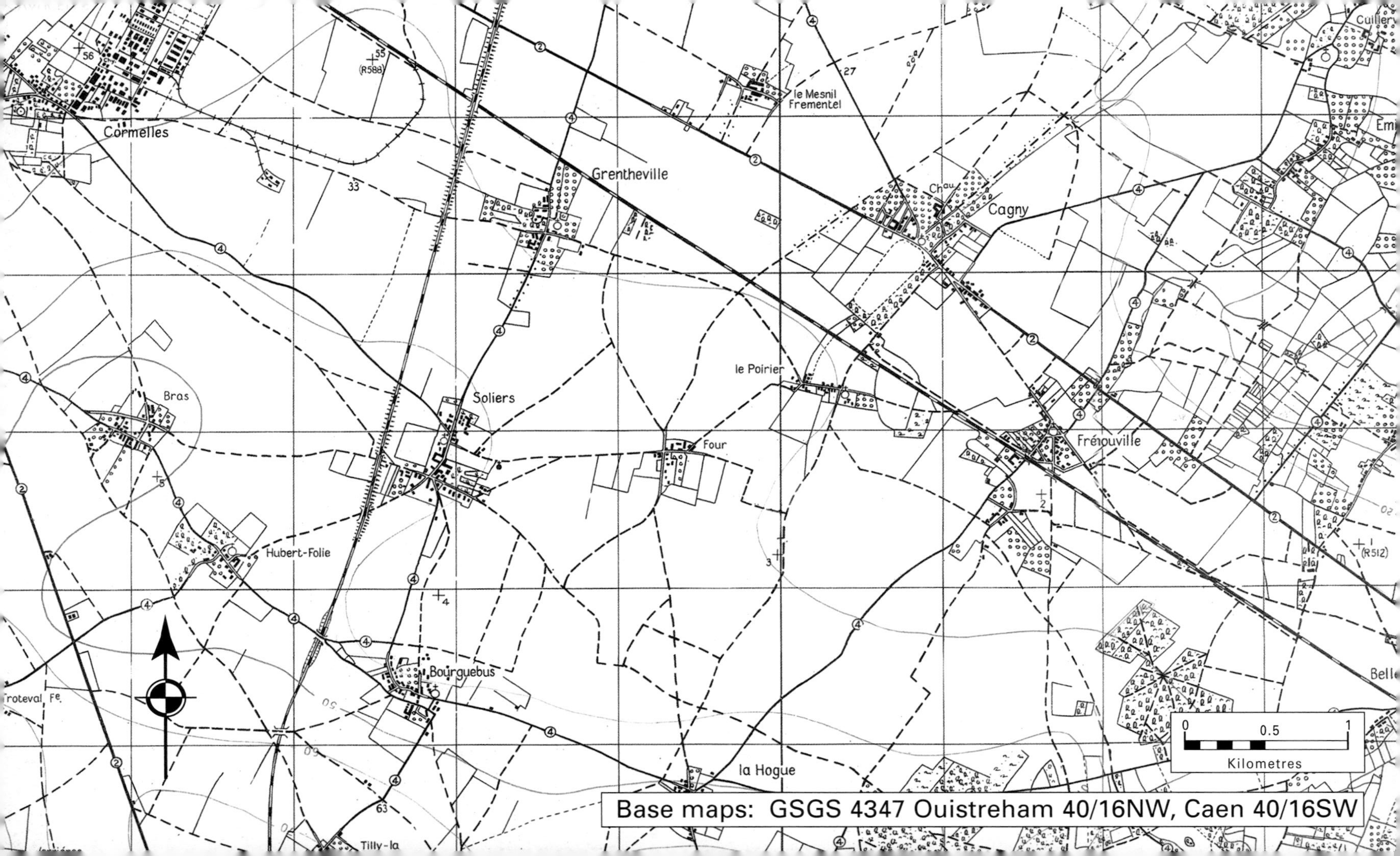
Cormelles
Grentheville
le Mesnil
Frementel
Cagny
Chau
Frénouville
le Poirier
Soliers
Four
Bras
Hubert-Folie
Bourguebus
la Hogue
Tilly-la
Troteval Fe.
(R588)
(R512)
0
0.5
1
Kilometres
Base maps: GSGS 4347 Ouistreham 40/16NW, Caen 40/16SW

to fight, or sometimes even to stand, and both Cuverville and the orchard were captured before 1020 hours. Démouville was secured by 1500 hours with help from the leading troops of 32nd Guards Brigade by then arriving in the area.

Canadian infantry of the North Nova Scotia Highlanders (9th Brigade) move forward, watched by an officer. *(NAC PA-141709)*

Operation Atlantic began at 0815 hours with its rolling artillery barrage, and at 0830 hours 8th Canadian Infantry Brigade supported by 2nd Canadian Armoured Brigade crossed its start line and advanced into Colombelles, with 9th Canadian Infantry Brigade moving across 'London' bridge behind them. Although the heavy bombing had ended here at 0604 hours, Le Régiment de la Chaudière took the village without much difficulty against I/32nd *Luftwaffe* Rifles. To the east the Queen's Own Rifles continued to make good progress, reaching the outskirts of Giberville by about 1100 hours. Shermans of the 1st Hussars knocked out several self-propelled guns; others escaped south from Colombelles, moving to the west of the steeply embanked rail line which effectively divided the western part of the battlefield from the fighting to the east.

Nearer the Orne, Le Régiment de la Chaudière advanced through the park belonging to Colombelles château, meeting resistance from I/192nd Panzergrenadiers and I/32nd *Luftwaffe* Rifles. By noon the North Shore Regiment, and also the Glens leading 9th Canadian Infantry Brigade, had become involved in this battle, but within four hours the Canadians had by-passed and captured the château. At 1645 hours Maj-Gen Keller issued orders for the North Shore Regiment to continue the fight for the steelworks and the Queen's Own Rifles for Giberville, while 9th Brigade pushed on for Vaucelles.

In the centre the troops of II/32nd and I/46th *Luftwaffe* Rifles, under fire from 29th Armoured Brigade as it crossed the start line behind VIII Corps barrage at 0745 hours, were also stunned by the bombing and surrendered in large numbers. In 20 minutes 3rd RTR had reached the Caen–Troarn railway line and ten minutes later even 23rd Hussars was clear of the British minefield. Problems with the minefield, the railway line, and fire from the recovering Germans caused the advance to slip slightly behind schedule. When the barrage resumed at 0845 hours, rolling south-westerly from 300 metres south of the railway line towards le Mesnil Frémentel farm, 2nd Fife and Forfar Yeomanry had still not quite come up level to the east of 3rd RTR, and neither battalion was as close to the barrage as it wished. But 23rd Hussars were also across the rail line before 0930 hours, and the advance began to make up lost time.

After 11th Armoured Division had completed its crossing, 5th Guards Armoured Brigade began to cross at 'York' and 'Euston' bridges at 0834 hours (not 0800 as originally planned) and turned southwards. At 0945 hours the brigade's last vehicles were still crossing the bridges, while 6 km to the south near Démouville its leading tanks were closing up on 29th Armoured Brigade. The delay in turn affected 22nd Armoured Brigade; its leading battalion, 5th RTR in its Cromwells, began to cross 'London' bridge almost perfectly on time at 0847 hours, only to be held up behind 9th Canadian Infantry Brigade moving south towards Colombelles, and then behind both Guards and 11th Armoured Divisions. By midday, 5th RTR was still the only battalion of 7th Armoured Division to have completed crossing, to the increasing worry of VIII Corps' staff. At 1340 hours Lt-Gen O'Connor ordered 7th Armoured Division to rush the battalions of 22nd Armoured Brigade southwards individually to reinforce 29th Armoured Brigade, rather than waiting for the whole brigade to get past the increasing traffic jam between the Orne bridges and the start line.

To the east of 11th Armoured Division's break-through, 3rd British Infantry Division, including 27th Armoured Brigade and 152nd (Highland) Brigade, also began its attack at 0745 hours behind the artillery barrage. This was much more of a set-piece attack, south-eastwards with 8th Infantry Brigade, its northern flank covered by 152nd (Highland) Brigade, and then 9th Infantry Brigade coming through to capture Troarn, while 185th Infantry Brigade attacked southwards to capture Guillerville and Émiéville, protecting the flank of VIII Corps' advance.

Soldiers of 3rd Irish Guards, well protected against the dust thrown up by VIII Corps' advance, await the order to move forward, 18 July. *(IWM B7533)*

8th Infantry Brigade, supported by 13th/18th Hussars, was soon locked in heavy fighting in the woods with 857th Grenadiers. By 1100 hours, 2nd East Yorkshires had reached Touffréville, partly missed by the bombing, and it took another hard fight until the evening to capture the village and its woods along with 90 prisoners. But to the south the bombing had done its job and the Germans were ready to surrender; by about midday, 1st Suffolks had captured the rubble of Sannerville, followed by Banneville-la-Campagne. 152nd (Highland) Brigade at first used flame-throwing Churchill Crocodile tanks of B Squadron, 141st RAC, to burn out the defenders of I/46th *Luftwaffe* Rifles, and then engaged in a protracted fight for the ruins of a nearby château that lasted until the evening. Soon after the Highlanders started their advance, 185th Infantry Brigade moved off southwards, led by 2nd KSLI riding on the Shermans of the Staffordshire Yeomanry, and by 1430 hours it had captured the hamlet of Lirose, just north of the Caen–Troarn railway line and west of Sannerville.

The northern edge of Sannerville, seen from the modern D226. 1st Suffolks attacked astride the road, capturing the orchard on the left and then moving south to consolidate the village. *(SCT)*

Meanwhile, in the centre, 29th Armoured Brigade's advance towards the N13 road and the second railway line continued. By 0915 hours the leading tanks were past le Prieuré farm with its orchard and closing on le Mesnil Frémentel. The British tanks took some losses as German anti-tank guns opened fire, but had orders to push on rather than halt to deal with small pockets of resistance. Two batteries of 200th Assault Gun Battalion pulled back south behind Cagny, 4/200th to its new position near le Poirier farm, and 5/200th circling around Cagny from the east and possibly stopping there briefly, then on to the hamlet of Four. Within ten minutes, 3rd RTR and 2nd Fife and Forfar Yeomanry had by-passed le Mesnil Frémentel to west and east respectively, and the leading tanks were up to the Caen–Vimont railway line. Like other walled farms and villages, le Mesnil Frémentel had to be captured house-to-house; a mixed force including Sherman Crab flail tanks of A and B Squadrons, 22nd Dragoons, and troops of 8th Rifle Brigade secured the farm by 1130 hours, but took much of the day to round up 134 prisoners. The unsupported garrison of le Prieuré farm later surrendered to the Guards Armoured Division.

As 2nd Fife and Forfar Yeomanry advanced past Cagny its rearmost C Squadron and part of B Squadron were hit by fire from the east, including shots from the 88-mm *Luftwaffe* Flak battery in the village, hastily organised into an anti-tank role by *Major* von Luck of 21st Panzer Division, who had returned from leave in Paris that morning. By his own vivid account, von Luck then single-handedly set about restoring the German defence to the south-east. Even so, by 0946 hours 3rd RTR and most of 2nd Fife and Forfar Yeomanry were over the Caen–Vimont railway line and advancing on up Bourguébus ridge, only six minutes behind schedule and 16 minutes after the last bombs had hit the German gun line.

Now the problem was not Cagny as expected but Grentheville to the west, unscathed by the bombing, and the lack of enough British infantry to deal with the German artillery and anti-tank guns. Exchanging heavy fire with the troops and assault guns in the village and the nearby 75-mm Pak detachment, 3rd RTR skirted westwards, shooting up some batteries of 14th Werfer Regiment in the open, and taking its own first losses. By 1000 hours the Shermans had evaded the German fire by crossing under and over the embanked railway that ran south from Colombelles. With the solid obstacle of the steep 3–4 metre railway embankment between themselves and Grentheville, 3rd RTR's tanks continued west towards Cormelles on the outskirts of industrial Caen. They then turned southward towards Bras and Hubert-Folie, where the local garrison was being joined by those guns of 2/200th Assault Gun Battalion that had escaped south along the railway embankment from Giberville.

Meanwhile, 2nd Fife and Forfar Yeomanry, which had already lost at least 12 tanks west of Cagny, carried on southward, reaching Soliers and nearby Four where the battalion came under artillery and anti-tank fire from the German gun line, taking more losses. In a matter of minutes, what had been planned as an attack by three armoured divisions onto the Bourguébus ridge had become unsupported advances into heavy fire by two battalions of tanks, out of sight of each other and separated by a major obstacle.

Just as the first tanks were climbing the slopes of Bourguébus ridge, *General* Eberbach, who got no clear reports from the old

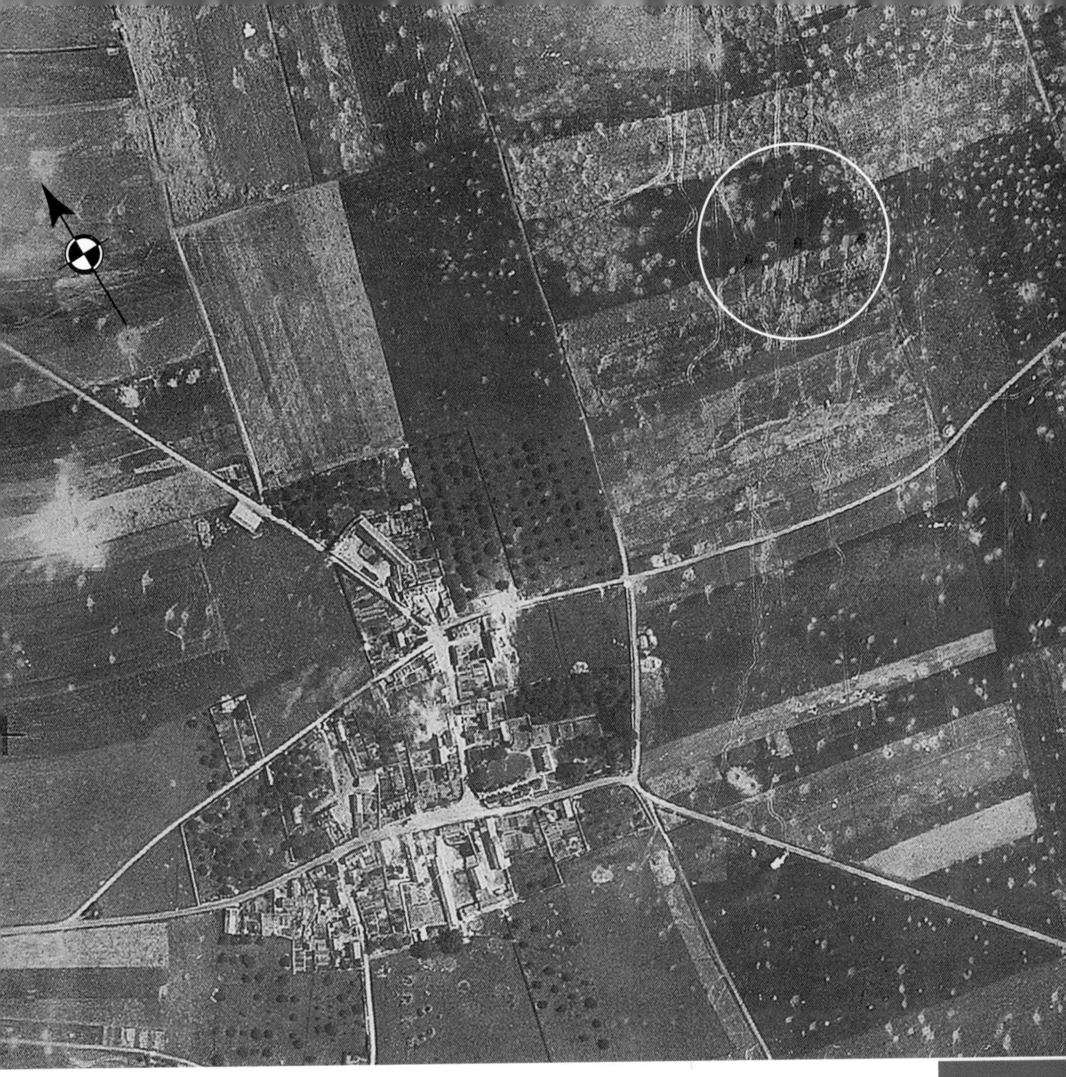

Bras (*bottom left*), seen from the air at approximately 1200 hours on 18 July. A troop of 3rd RTR Shermans (*circled*) can be seen withdrawing from the edge of the village, while several other tanks (including at least two that appear to have been knocked out) can be seen nearby. *(Keele University Air Photo Archive)*

German front line all day, ordered Sepp Dietrich, whose first concern was the attack by II Canadian Corps within his own I SS Panzer Corps sector, to send the *Leibstandarte* Division north-east onto the Bourguébus ridge, including the Panzer IVs of II/1st SS Panzers and 1st SS Assault Gun Battalion from corps reserve west of the Orne. (Dietrich may also have sent any operational Tigers of 101st Heavy SS Panzer Battalion.) This was not a defensive move but a full armoured charge over the ridge and through Cagny to coincide with an attack from the east by 21st Panzer Division that Eberbach had also ordered, not knowing what the bombing had done. This double encirclement was planned to hit both sides of what the Germans expected to be the main line of the British attack south-eastwards through Vimont, driving it back to the Caen–Troarn rail line and recovering the original battle zone in classic German tactical style. At 1720 hours Field Marshal von Kluge at OB West confirmed these orders.

Making their way along minor roads and evading Allied fighter-bombers, the tanks and troops of the *Leibstandarte* Division entered the battle for Bourguébus ridge piecemeal. The exact times that each unit arrived are unclear, particularly as the British identified almost any vehicle they saw as a Tiger or Panther. It is just possible that a few Tigers from 101st Heavy SS Panzer Battalion took part in the first defence of Bras and Hubert-Folie against 3rd RTR. The British battalion lost tanks repeatedly as it tried to advance against the two villages, including to fire from the village of Ifs almost 1.8 km westward. A few Shermans of 3rd RTR managed to get past the village to the east and even across the road to Bourguébus before being forced back. While 23rd Hussars and 8th Rifle Brigade dealt with Grentheville, 2nd Fife and Forfar Yeomanry also got a few tanks across the ridge road (the modern D89) near Bourguébus by 1115 hours, but they were repeatedly pinned down and forced back beyond Soliers by anti-tank fire, including shots coming from behind them from near Frénouville. All over the lower northern slopes of the Bourguébus ridge, British tanks were stationary, knocked out or burning fiercely.

The first Panthers of I/1st SS Panzers arrived on the ridge probably just after noon, and soon the British were reporting German guns and tanks everywhere. Choking dust and smoke, some of it from burning crops, added to the confusion. At about 1215 hours the air controller with 29th Armoured Brigade was wounded, but his Army deputy soon took over directing Typhoon rocket strikes onto the ridge. Although the British did not realise it, these directed strikes all afternoon were vital in delaying or breaking up the *Leibstandarte* Division's counter-attacks.

3rd RTR and 2nd Fife and Forfar Yeomanry were still greatly in need of support, as individual tanks or small groups advanced or retreated into and out of range of the German guns. But, as they came forward past le Prieuré farm to help, the tanks of 23rd Hussars were fired upon from the east by a few Tigers of 3/503rd Heavy Panzer Battalion emerging from near Manneville stud farm and took cover. The Tigers advanced almost up to le Prieuré before falling back after unexpectedly losing two tanks, possibly from the 88-mm Flak guns at Cagny firing at the wrong target.

View from the D228 bridge over the A-13 motorway, looking south-east towards le Prieuré farm (*centre, behind the pylon*). On 18 July almost all of VIII Corps' armour had to squeeze through the area shown here in order to continue its advance south. *(SCT)*

The early appearance of these Tigers posed a threat to the British out of all proportion to their numbers, distracting 5th Guards Armoured Brigade from helping 29th Armoured Brigade, and bringing the southward advance of 185th Infantry Brigade to a halt north of Manneville. The overall result was to squeeze Guards Armoured Division's advance away westward from its planned route, increasing the traffic jam delaying 7th Armoured Division behind it. At 1040 hours 2nd (Armoured) Grenadier Guards, lacking infantry and with orders not to attack Cagny if there was a strong garrison, halted north of the village. Other than the 88-mm *Luftwaffe* battery, the exact strength of the Cagny garrison cannot be determined; *Major* von Luck believed that for much of the day the village was undefended, but this is most unlikely. At the same time, 1st (Armoured) Coldstream Guards came under attack from King Tigers of 1/503rd Heavy Panzer Battalion (and possibly some Panzer IVs of 22nd Panzer) that also emerged from near Manneville. Again, concentrated British fire forced the German tanks to retreat.

A heavily camouflaged 88-mm Pak 43. The arrival of almost 30 such guns to reinforce the German front on 18 July ensured there would be no breakthrough towards Vimont. *(BA 720/315/5a)*

Around midday, LXXXVI Corps strengthened its line facing north-west between Frénouville and Émiéville with some 88-mm Pak guns of 1039th Anti-Tank Battalion, and by redeploying the surviving Tigers and the Panzer IVs of 21st Panzer Division from the east to the south-east. 1st (Armoured) Coldstream Guards was unable to continue on past Frénouville to Vimont in the face of their fire, and at 1230 hours the battalion was ordered to retreat behind 2nd (Armoured) Grenadier Guards and circle all the way round Cagny from the north and west, further blocking the route through the centre. The Panzer IVs of II/1st SS Panzers joined the Panthers on the ridge, but 29th Armoured Brigade never truly became aware of a massed German attempt to counter-attack downslope, being more worried by its own inability to get forward. With so much fire being exchanged, neither side was in a position to attack decisively, but with their inferior tanks and exposed positions the British were getting the worst of it.

By mid-afternoon, 29th Armoured Brigade's attack on Bourguébus ridge had spent itself in knocked out and burning tanks. About 25 surviving tanks of 2nd Fife and Forfar Yeomanry had pulled back through 23rd Hussars and north of the Caen–Vimont railway line to regroup. At 1535 hours Maj-Gen Roberts ordered 3rd RTR, which was losing almost as heavily, to withdraw only if essential, reinforcing it with the Cromwells of 2nd Northamptonshire Yeomanry, which also took losses from Bras and Hubert-Folie, including from the newly-arrived 1st SS Assault Gun Battalion. Whatever they did, the British tanks could not get forward.

At 1350 hours 32nd Guards Brigade in its lorries was ordered to move from Démouville and prepare to attack Cagny. By 1445 hours, 1st (Armoured) Coldstream Guards had also completed its circle round Cagny and advanced south-eastward down the second railway line, coming under assault-gun fire from le Poirier before the Guards' Shermans captured it at 1630 hours. 2nd (Armoured) Irish Guards also came into action on the eastern flank, and in one celebrated episode north-east of Cagny a Sherman actually rammed a King Tiger that had become separated from its company (*see Tour D, pp. 175–7*). At the end of the day 503rd Heavy Panzer Battalion reported only nine tanks still operational.

The Guards Armoured Division plaque, Cagny church. *(SCT)*

At last, at 1800 hours in a brief rainstorm, The King's Company of 1st (Motorised) Grenadier Guards attached to 2nd (Armoured) Grenadier Guards entered Cagny from the north, supported by 5th Coldstream Guards, and by 1930 hours the village had been cleared of all resistance. Shortly after Cagny was captured, 2nd (Armoured Reconnaissance) Welsh Guards joined 2nd (Armoured) Irish Guards to the north, holding most of the Manneville stud farm area; but neither Guards battalion could get further east or south-east.

With 5th Guards Armoured Brigade tied up before Cagny, 5th RTR (leading 22nd Armoured Brigade) crossed the Caen–Troarn rail line at 1545 hours and reached Grentheville by 1700 hours, followed by 1st RTR. Within an hour 5th RTR was exchanging long-range fire with German 'tanks' from Four, but it remained the only battalion of 7th Armoured Division to get into action that day. At 1830 hours, as 23rd Hussars advanced across the Caen–Vimont rail line between Grentheville and le Poirier, they ran into a major counter-attack downslope by the Panthers of I/1st SS Panzer, organised by *SS-Obergruppenführer* Wisch. In the exchange of fire C Squadron, 23rd Hussars, lost most of its tanks, but I/1st SS Panzer also lost several tanks and retreated.

By 1945 hours, 29th Armoured Brigade had been ordered to rally back and 'harbour' for the night. Maj-Gen Roberts also ordered 159th Infantry Brigade forward to just north of le Mesnil Frémentel, which it reached by 2000 hours. Even north of the Caen–Vimont railway line, the British tanks were still within long range from Soliers, and a heavy artillery concentration was brought down on the village (reported by the British as full of Tigers and Panthers) at 2030 hours to block what was probably the day's last attempt at a counter-attack by the *Leibstandarte* Division. Tanks continued to exchange shots as the sun set, with the British still coming off worst; 3rd RTR claimed two German tanks but lost six of its own as the light faded. It had been a terrible day for the British armour. Roberts later gave his losses as 126 tanks out of 244 (286 including Stuarts), including more than 40 each from 3rd RTR and 2nd Fife and Forfar Yeomanry.

At 2000 hours III/1st SS Panzergrenadiers joined the defenders of Bras, and in the course of the night the rest of 1st SS Panzergrenadiers took up the line as far east as Bourguébus village, then 2nd SS Panzergrenadiers continuing through Soliers to la Hogue. The *Hitlerjugend* Division was returned to I SS Panzer Corps' command at 1520 hours, and was ordered to move up and take over the sector from Émiéville to Frénouville, with its battlegroups arriving early on 19 July and releasing 21st Panzer Division to concentrate on defending Troarn. Units of 711th Infantry Division, a D-Day division that was partly refitting near Lisieux, were also sent to the defence of Troarn; the first of these, III/731st Infantry, arrived on bicycles on 19 July.

On the flanks of the main VIII Corps attack most but not all of the objectives set by Second Army were captured in the course of 18 July. In Operation Atlantic, the North Nova Scotia Regiment and HLI of Canada successfully by-passed Colombelles steelworks along the riverbank, and reached Vaucelles before sunset against very little opposition as II/980th Grenadiers fell back rather than be cut off by 11th Armoured Division's advance. West of the Orne, 4th Canadian Infantry Brigade from 2nd

Canadian Infantry Division attacked southwards towards the village of Louvigny but was held up by I/980th Grenadiers. At 1715 hours 7th Canadian Infantry Brigade started to cross the Orne into Vaucelles, and at last light 5th Canadian Infantry Brigade also began crossing. Through the night 2nd Canadian Infantry Division continued to build bridges across the Orne into Vaucelles under considerable German mortar and artillery fire. To the north, the fight by 8th Canadian Infantry Brigade at Colombelles steelworks and Giberville also continued on into the night. The last radio transmission from I/192nd Panzergrenadiers in the ruins of the steelworks was 'Battalion Headquarters surrounded. *Heil der Führer!*' In the climate of the times, this dramatic phrase in various forms was used unofficially to signal an unauthorised retreat, and I/192nd Grenadiers reached the safety of the ridge after nightfall. By 2130 hours Giberville was also in Canadian hands with 200 prisoners, although fighting in the area continued on into the next day.

200th Assault Gun Battalion helped repulse VIII Corps' attack on 18 July, but paid a heavy price in men and vehicles. The original caption identifies this destroyed self-propelled gun as being found at Mondeville, suggesting that it belonged to the battalion's 2nd Battery. *(IWM B7752)*

Soldiers of 3rd Infantry Division, accompanied by Sherman tanks from 27th Armoured Brigade, advance on 18 July. *(IWM B7553)*

On the eastern flank, 3rd British Infantry Division had failed to capture Troarn, not knowing that for LXXXVI Corps its defence was a critical objective, but had succeeded in protecting the flank of VIII Corps' advance. At 1600 hours, 9th Infantry Brigade, supported by the tanks of the East Riding Yeomanry, passed through 8th Infantry Brigade at Sannerville and advanced across the swampy ground and up the slope towards Troarn with 1st King's Own Scottish Borderers and 2nd Royal Ulster Rifles leading, meeting stiff opposition from 858th Grenadiers, who still held the British in the dense orchards 2 km west of Troarn by nightfall. 185th Infantry Brigade had worked its way southwards and at 2100 hours 2nd Warwicks attacked Guillerville, capturing it with 40 prisoners against heavy German shelling just before midnight. Second Army's new front line now ran from Touffréville through Guillerville south to Cagny and west to Grentheville, and then south-west to Vaucelles and the Orne.

Despite the Allied domination of the skies, the *Luftwaffe* responded to the threat of a break-out east of Caen with a maximum effort. At 2330 hours medium bombers – probably Junkers 88s – put in a rare attack lit by flares on the Orne bridgehead. Euston bridge was slightly damaged, 11th Armoured Division headquarters was hit, and a number of tank crews who had survived the day became casualties. For the next two days, troops attacking Bourguébus ridge were surprised to be strafed by small formations of Messerschmitt Bf 109 fighters that had broken through the Allied air cover, sometimes at critical moments.

CHAPTER 5

THE LAST BATTLES

The morning of 19 July was partly overcast with some rain, and Montgomery was content to declare victory and close the battle down to avoid taking more casualties. At 0930 hours on 19 July, Dempsey visited VIII Corps headquarters and issued new orders for a limited advance, and even these objectives were further scaled down all the way along the British chain of command.

The rest of 7th Armoured Division, led by 131st (Queen's) Infantry Brigade, had finally crossed the Orne bridges, but would take most of the morning to make its way south through what was still a very congested bridgehead. 11th Armoured Division also needed the morning to reorganise. At 1035 hours Lt-Gen O'Connor met his three divisional commanders, and together they agreed a plan for a series of set-piece attacks starting at 1600 hours that afternoon, aimed solely at capturing the villages that had eluded them on the previous day. With VIII Corps artillery and the infantry brigades moving up to join the tanks, these villages would become death traps for the Germans; but after their losses of 18 July neither 11th Armoured Division nor Guards Armoured Division would attempt more.

The Germans still feared a powerful British attack south-east towards Paris, possibly starting again with the dreaded heavy bombers. (These had in fact been allocated to Operation Cobra, originally scheduled for 19 July; but Cobra had now been delayed until 24 July, chiefly by strong German resistance at

Then: A Sherman of 13/18th Royal Hussars (27th Armoured Brigade) heads west along the N175 in front of the ruins of Sannerville Château, 19 July. *(IWM B7684)*

Now: A modern view of the repaired château. *(SCT)*

St-Lô.) Field Marshal von Kluge moved to Rommel's headquarters at la Roche-Guyon to take over command of Army Group B as well as OB West, issuing orders for the *Leibstandarte* Division to continue its encirclement of this expected British drive, with 21st Panzer Division joining in from the east and the *Hitlerjugend* Division from the south-east. These counter-attacks, which barely got beyond their start lines against British firepower, played into Montgomery's hands by tying down and using up the German armoured reserves, but did inflict further casualties on the British and Canadians. The delay to Operation Cobra also meant a continued need to keep the Panzers engaged against Second Army. It took another week of hard fighting, particularly for 2nd Canadian Division and 3rd British Infantry Division on the flanks, before the battle for Caen was truly over.

The first small counter-attacks by the *Leibstandarte* Division down the slope of the Bourguébus ridge started at 0700 hours; most were beaten off, but one company of 2nd SS Panzergrenadiers managed to recapture le Poirier. After this, the *Leibstandarte* concentrated on strengthening the positions it already held, drawing back from the more vulnerable villages. Moving up at first light, 22nd Armoured Brigade found Soliers weakly defended, and by midday it had cleared the village. Battlegroup *Waldmüller* of the *Hitlerjugend* Division arrived from near Falaise to take over at Vimont and Frénouville at 0530 hours, and by midday Battlegroup *Wünsche* from Lisieux had come into line joined by Jagdpanzer IV tank destroyers of 1/12th SS Panzerjäger Battalion, with III/26th SS Panzergrenadiers taking over the defence of Émiéville.

To the west, 272nd Infantry Division gave up each village east of the Orne as the Canadians advanced, and then brought down mortar and artillery fire on its old positions. Starting at 0400 hours, 3rd Canadian Infantry Division secured Colombelles and Giberville and resumed clearing Vaucelles of the remaining snipers, machine guns and minefields of II/980th Grenadiers, an operation that took most of the day. 4th Canadian Infantry Brigade also renewed its attack against Louvigny, capturing it by just after 1100 hours. That night the brigade was relieved by 129th Infantry Brigade of 43rd (Wessex) Division as part of a general shift of II Canadian Corps eastwards across the Orne to take over ground gained by VIII Corps.

On the east side of the river, by 1130 hours the bridges at

Vaucelles were completed, and at 1600 hours the HLI of Canada captured Cormelles. 5th Canadian Infantry Brigade supported by armour attacked southwards along the east bank of the Orne to Fleury-sur-Orne and captured it by 1430 hours. Its leading battalion, the Calgary Highlanders, went on to reach Point 67, about 2 km south of the village, by 1715 hours, and dug in against the inevitable mortaring and counter-attacks. Ifs, the next village to the east, was attacked at last light by the Black Watch of Canada, but not fully captured until the following morning.

Canadian casualties of Operation Atlantic are evacuated from Vaucelles, 20 July. *(NAC PA-129031)*

At 0700 hours on 19 July, 3rd British Infantry Division resumed its attack eastwards towards Troarn through the dense orchards, using only 9th Infantry Brigade in what Second Army saw as a continuing secondary operation in a battle that was winding down, but that Panzer Group West perceived as the northern arm of the main British offensive to be thrown back at all costs. The result was similar to that of Operation Windsor against Carpiquet three weeks earlier, with 9th Infantry Brigade being raked by German crossfire. By evening all three battalions had taken heavy casualties, 2nd Lincolns fighting for what they called the 'black orchard', and the brigade was still 800 metres short of its objective of Troarn railway station. A little further south, 185th Infantry Brigade captured the undefended Manneville stud farm during the morning. At 1930 hours, armour and infantry of the *Hitlerjugend* Division mounted a counter-attack against Manneville supported by artillery, but were driven off.

The main VIII Corps attacks on 19 July began late in the afternoon as planned. Around 1600 hours, 11th Armoured Division artillery opened fire on Bras, now held by III/1st SS Panzergrenadiers with some assault guns (including elements of 200th Assault Gun Battalion, separated from the rest of 21st Panzer Division). After ten minutes 29th Armoured Brigade attacked the village with 2nd Northamptonshire Yeomanry, followed by 3rd RTR, the dismounted infantry of 8th Rifle Brigade, and 3rd Monmouths from 159th Infantry Brigade, capturing it by 1740 hours with 250 prisoners. Soon after 1800 hours, 3rd Monmouths took over the village, and 2nd Northamptonshire Yeomanry made a quick attempt to continue from Bras south-east up the ridge through the high crops to Hubert-Folie. Against the troops of I/1st SS Panzergrenadiers and their supporting armour the attack failed, with the loss of 37 tanks out of the 65 lost by 11th Armoured Division that day. At 2000 hours 2nd Fife and Forfar Yeomanry together with a company of 8th Rifle Brigade renewed the attack with heavy fire support including from all nearby tanks. At 2045 hours, against all expectations, 18 Messerschmitt Bf 109 fighters flew low over the battlefield and strafed 159th Infantry Brigade's supporting advance; but within half an hour I/1st SS Panzergrenadiers had been driven out of the village which was captured with 50 prisoners, although the Germans again responded by shelling and mortaring it heavily. By nightfall 159th Infantry Brigade was dug in at Hubert-Folie, while 29th Armoured Brigade harboured north of Grentheville.

7th Armoured Division's main attack began at 1700 hours towards Four and Bourguébus, also with strong artillery support. Four was captured at 2045 hours by 1st RTR and 1st Rifle Brigade, with the aid of petard mortar fire from an Armoured Vehicle Royal Engineers (AVRE) of 26th Assault Squadron, RE. At 1840 hours 5th RTR reported the defence of Bourguébus as including two Panthers and three Tigers, while other troops of 2nd SS Panzergrenadiers provided crossfire from la Hogue. The attack continued, and by 2045 hours 5th RTR had Bourguébus surrounded, while a bombing attack by Typhoons on la Hogue at 2155 hours at least enabled its tanks to get astride the road between the two villages, but the Germans continued to hold them both.

After early morning patrols revealed that the Germans would defend Émiéville and Vimont in strength, Guards Armoured Division's main effort on 19 July went into reorganising and linking up with 3rd British Infantry Division to the north. At 1700 hours 1st Welsh Guards recaptured le Poirier without much difficulty as the SS Panzergrenadiers fell back to Four, but no plans were made to take Frénouville until next day. Instead the two sides sniped at each other with long range tank and anti-tank fire. Nevertheless, by nightfall on 19 July, *Major* von Luck was convinced that 21st Panzer Division had helped defeat a serious assault by both the Guards Armoured Division and 7th Armoured Division towards Vimont and the south-east that in fact had never happened.

At 0545 hours (dawn) on 20 July, elements of the Guards Armoured Division attacked Frénouville to find that the *Hitlerjugend* had abandoned the village during the night to shorten its line. 7th Armoured Division also renewed its attack on Bourguébus at 0545 hours to find that the *Leibstandarte* Division had also pulled back to the next village upslope, Tilly-la-Campagne. At 1000 hours, 3rd Canadian Infantry Division relieved 11th Armoured Division, including at Bras and Hubert-Folie. A German counter-attack at Bras with seven tanks, possibly Tigers, as this relief took place caused a small crisis, but by midday the village was securely in Canadian hands.

For VIII Corps and its armoured divisions, Operation Goodwood was over. The whole of Caen including Vaucelles and its outlying villages had been liberated, and the routes around the town were open to Allied movement. But this was far removed from the break-out to reach Falaise which SHAEF had expected. At 1620 hours on 18 July, after giving a jubilant press conference, Montgomery had signalled Field Marshal Brooke that the morning's operations were 'a complete success'. At 2000 hours Second Army's main headquarters had (apparently unknown to Lt-Gen Dempsey) informed 21st Army Group and First US Army

Soldiers of 1st Welsh Guards in action near Cagny on 19 July. The photo was probably taken in the afternoon, during the attack on le Poirier. *(IWM B7759)*

that, 'By mid-day strong armoured formations of VIII Corps had advanced nearly seven miles [11 km] to the south and had broken through the main German defences.' In fact scout cars of the Inns of Court Regiment *had* got completely over the ridge and explored 'for several miles southward' down the Caen–Falaise road. At 1400 hours on 19 July, Brooke, who had flown over to Normandy in response to Churchill's outburst the day before, found Montgomery 'delighted with his success east of Caen', and that evening Montgomery sent another jubilant signal to Eisenhower. Churchill, who visited Montgomery on 21 July, also found him more than content. The story of a British break-through was repeated by SHAEF headquarters in England to Allied journalists, though Montgomery and Dempsey both later hinted that this was all a cover plan to mislead the Germans that Second Army still intended to attack south-eastwards for Paris.

As the true picture of a limited advance that had not even cleared the whole of Bourguébus ridge emerged, a furious Eisenhower flew to Normandy on 20 July to see Montgomery. He was greeted with news picked up by 21st Army Group radios: Hitler might be dead. At 1342 hours (local time) an assassin's bomb had exploded at the OKW 'Wolf's Lair' headquarters near Rastenburg in eastern Germany, planted by *Oberst* (Colonel) Klaus Schenk Graf von Stauffenberg. At least temporarily, Montgomery and Caen were no longer Eisenhower's chief concern. Hitler survived the bomb blast and, as the news of his survival spread, the plot against him collapsed. Secret orders to *Heer* units forcibly to disarm the *Waffen-SS* troops now fighting alongside them on Bourguébus ridge and at Vimont were quickly hidden. For the senior officers of Panzer Group West this was not the time to question orders or show lack of aggression.

A large part of the argument over Operation Goodwood, as with all of the battle for Caen, has fixed on casualties and tank losses suffered by both sides, of which no conclusive assessment can ever be made. VIII Corps and I Corps took just over 2,000 Germans prisoner during 18–20 July, 700 of them taken by 3rd British Infantry Division and even more by 11th Armoured Division; II Canadian Corps also took its share. At least 500 of these prisoners came from 21st Panzer Division, which was pulled out of the line to be rebuilt. The luckless 16th *Luftwaffe* Field Division lost 900 prisoners to the British and Canadians, and was broken up after the battle, some of its troops and equipment going to 21st Panzer Division. 346th Infantry Division lost half its infantry and over a third of its artillery and anti-tank guns defending Troarn. Records of casualties for the *Leibstandarte* Division for this period have not survived, but losses included more than 200 prisoners captured by the British in Bras and Hubert-Folie on 19 July. The *Hitlerjugend* Division, which was much less heavily involved in the battle, recorded only 134 casualties between 19 July and 4 August, including 18 dead.

Prime Minister Churchill visits Montgomery's headquarters, 21 July. Although the meeting contributed to a thaw in their relationship, the tension of the moment is evident on the faces of both men. *(IWM B7769)*

German losses in equipment included 47 launchers from 9th Werfer Brigade. In 21st Panzer Division, 22nd Panzer Regiment lost 28 tanks completely destroyed or abandoned, and 503rd Heavy Panzer Battalion lost eight. The *Waffen-SS* tank and assault gun battalions recorded only losses that were not replaced 18–22 July: II/1st SS Panzers lost 20 out of 61 Panzer IVs; 1st SS Assault Gun Battalion lost 17 out of 20 assault guns (although all but two were repairable); otherwise, replacements kept the battalions at about half strength of 20–35 operational vehicles each. 11th Armoured Division claimed to have disabled 16 German tanks 18–19 July (mostly described as 'Panthers') and destroyed 17, suggesting total German losses from all causes of perhaps 100 tanks.

Unlike the British, who could recover almost all their damaged tanks and return many to action, German tank losses in Operation Goodwood were gone forever. This Panzer IV, photographed near Cagny, was one of around 30 destroyed on 18 July. *(IWM B7760)*

The first estimates of Allied losses for Operation Goodwood appeared horrific, that Second Army had lost 4,011 men and 493 tanks. Numerous tanks had indeed been lost but usually their crews survived, and more than half of all tanks abandoned on 18 July were later recovered or repaired. VIII Corps lost 521 casualties on the 18th, including 81 men from the tank battalions of 11th Armoured Division and 79 from the tank units of Guards

Operation Goodwood ended in pouring rain and a sea of mud. Here a supply truck negotiates a flooded road, 21 July. *(IWM B7856)*

Armoured Division. 11th Armoured Division's four armoured battalions were the hardest hit, with 2nd Fife and Forfar Yeomanry losing 100 men killed and wounded (some from the *Luftwaffe* raid that night). After much investigation, estimates of tank losses for VIII Corps settled at 197 on 18 July, 99 more on 19 July and 18 on 20 July for a total of 314, of which 140 were completely destroyed, plus another 20 or so tanks in the flanking corps. The tank strength returns for VIII Corps 18–21 July show a loss of 218 tanks (that could not be repaired or immediately replaced), including 145 tanks from 11th Armoured Division.

Maj-Gen 'Bobbie' Erskine commanding 7th Armoured Division was one of two divisional generals removed from command later in July. Maj-Gen Allan Adair remained in command of Guards Armoured Division; as Montgomery later put it, 'General Allan was the only one that I knew I could never sack. My job was to fight the Germans. I wasn't prepared to fight the whole of the Brigade of Guards as well.'

In the wider battle for Normandy, what was important was that after nightfall on 18 July the last uncommitted Panzer division in northern France, 116th Panzer Division, was released to Panzer Group West for the Caen sector. Next evening

General Eberbach ordered armoured battlegroups of the *Hohenstaufen* and *Frundsberg* Divisions to move from the west of the Orne to the east, followed next day by Battlegroup *Köhn* from 2nd Panzer Division to take up reserve positions behind 272nd Infantry Division. Of the ten Panzer divisions in Army Group B when Operation Cobra began, eight were in Panzer Group West opposite Second Army, and the equivalent of five divisions were actually east of the Orne. According to Montgomery's own figures from 21st Army Group, about 190 German tanks opposed First US Army on 25 July and 645 tanks opposed the British and Canadians. The need to re-equip Panzer Group West after Goodwood took almost all of Army Group B's transport and supplies, leaving Seventh Army opposite the Americans critically short of fuel and shells when Cobra started. Also according to 21st Army Group figures, although the number of German infantry battalions facing the Americans increased 10–25 July from 72 to 85 (an increase equivalent to about two German infantry divisions), those opposite the British and Canadians increased from 65 to 92 (equivalent of about four divisions). The strategy of replacing Panzer divisions with infantry divisions around Caen in order to create an armoured reserve failed; the infantry arrived, but in winning the battle for Caen Montgomery had achieved his wider objective of 'writing down' the German armour, at considerable cost both to Second Army and to his own reputation with other Allied commanders.

Senior German officers were quite certain that at Caen they had suffered a catastrophic defeat: *General* Eberbach later described how, on 18 July, a wide hole had been torn in his line, and only closed with the greatest effort. Field Marshal von Kluge accepted after Caen that the battle of Normandy was lost. On 21 July he wrote to Hitler, 'the moment has drawn near when the front, already so heavily strained, will break'. Proved right by Operation Cobra a few days later, von Kluge was already under suspicion of involvement in the failed bomb plot. In August he committed suicide rather than face trial, followed by Rommel in October.

The main effort of Second Army's battle now switched to 2nd Canadian Division and Verrières ridge, where Lt-Gen Simonds continued with Operation Atlantic. With the capture of Bras, Hubert-Folie and Bourguébus, elements of 7th Armoured Division also attacked Verrières ridge from the east on 20 July, getting tanks across the Caen–Falaise road. But after discussion at army and corps level, 7th Armoured Division withdrew back east of the road at 1340 hours, leaving 2nd Canadian Division mostly to fight its own battle.

A French First World War veteran greets Canadians of the South Saskatchewan Regiment in Fleury-sur-Orne, 20 July. *(NAC PA-131386)*

At 1500 hours on 20 July, after Typhoon strikes and several hours of artillery exchanges, the reinforced 6th Canadian Infantry Brigade moved off from its start line just south of Point 67 through the tall wheat towards Verrières ridge and St-André-sur-Orne. On the ridge in front of the Canadians, battlegroups of the *Leibstandarte* Division were mixed in with 272nd Infantry Division. After an hour, a torrential summer rainstorm broke, turning the wheat fields into a muddy sea and filling slit trenches with water, preventing further air support and hampering artillery fire. The Queen's Own Cameron Highlanders of Canada reached St-André-sur-Orne by 1740 hours, secured the village and fought off the expected German counter-attack. But to the east at Beauvoir farm and Troteval farm Les Fusiliers Mont-Royal found itself in a hard fight with troops of 2nd SS Panzer-grenadiers and 1st SS Panzer Reconnaissance Battalion. By 2100 hours Les Fusiliers Mont-Royal had been forced downslope in the rain, and during the night the battalion lost two companies cut off and overrun. In the centre there was a catastrophe as two companies of 2nd SS Panzergrenadiers supported by assault guns counter-attacked behind a heavy concentration of artillery and mortar shells. The South Saskatchewan Regiment and part of the Essex Scottish were both overrun.

Next morning the weather cleared. Fierce fighting continued on both flanks, and in the centre the Essex Scottish, who had once again advanced, found themselves mixed in with German troops among the crops all day. At 1800 hours, the Black Watch of Canada, supported by Shermans of the 1st Hussars and Sherbrooke Fusiliers, made a successful attack to shore up the centre, fighting off a German counter-attack at 2100 hours. Through the night the Canadian positions were subject to more intense shelling, augmented by bombing and strafing from the *Luftwaffe*, and next day the *Leibstandarte* Division continued its counter-attacks, against St-André-sur-Orne and against Les Fusiliers Mont-Royal who had taken Troteval farm, each time being beaten back. The infantry and machine-gun battalions alone of 2nd Canadian Division took 1,149 casualties on 18–21 July, 824 of them in the battle in the rainstorm on 20–21 July including 215 South Saskatchewans and 244 Essex Scottish. Verrières ridge was to provoke even greater arguments for the Canadians than Bourguébus ridge for the British.

The fighting on Goodwood's eastern flank was costly and difficult, with German artillery and mortars taking a heavy toll. 2nd East Yorkshires, shown here, suffered 192 casualties before being withdrawn on 25 July. *(IWM B7683)*

On the eastern side of the battlefield on 20 July, after occupying Frénouville at dawn the Guards Armoured Division had a quiet day probing German positions near Émiéville and Vimont. What may have been the start of a *Hitlerjugend* Division attack from Émiéville at about 1115 hours was broken up by British artillery. On 3rd British Infantry Division front, 185th Infantry Brigade beat off another counter-attack by the *Hitlerjugend* from Émiéville towards Manneville in the afternoon. Late in the day, in the torrential rainstorm, 2nd Lincolns was again ordered to advance and occupy the 'black orchard' west of Troarn, where the men found that their slit trenches filled with mud and water as they dug. There was no German counter-attack, but the position was heavily shelled and mortared. The battalion lost over 200 killed and wounded over the two days, the majority to mortar fire in the last few hours of 20 July.

Early next morning patrols from 185th Infantry Brigade found Émiéville abandoned as the *Hitlerjugend* Division shortened its line to allow 21st Panzer Division to withdraw, and 2nd Royal Warwicks moved forward to occupy the village. 51st (Highland) Division came forward to take over the front at Cagny and Frénouville from the Guards Armoured Division, which withdrew into reserve, and 3rd Canadian Infantry Division took over the front on Bourguébus ridge from 7th Armoured Division. Late on 22 July, 5th Canadian Infantry Brigade captured the hamlet of Étavaux on the east bank of the Orne just north of St-André-sur-Orne, while 129th Infantry Brigade of 43rd (Wessex) Division captured Maltot village, a short distance west of the river, completing the junction south of Caen between XII Corps on the west side of the Orne and II Canadian Corps on the east side.

With the end of Operation Atlantic on 22 July, the battle for Caen was over, with a victory for Second Army. The last battles had been hard fought ones: Second Army's casualties for 18–22 July were 5,088 men. I Corps and II Canadian Corps each lost almost as many men as VIII Corps, the consequence of the continued German counter-attacks and of 2nd Canadian Infantry Division's attacks southwards after 18 July. The three infantry divisions on both flanks during Operation Goodwood/Atlantic all lost substantially more men than the three armoured divisions in the centre, 2,710 casualties altogether compared to 1,241, and in all six British and Canadian divisions that took part average losses among the infantry battalions at 9 per cent were about

Canadian troops move forward from Vaucelles on 25 July to participate in Operation Spring. The attack ended in failure when battlegroups of I SS Panzer Corps counter-attacked, inflicting terrible casualties on several Canadian regiments and recapturing a number of villages. *(NAC PA-131378)*

twice as high as for the armoured battalions. Lt-Gen Dempsey's assessment to the reporter Chester Wilmot that, 'I was prepared to lose a couple of hundred tanks, so long as I didn't lose men', was good strategy for the British, although Dempsey's added remark that, 'our tank losses were severe but our casualties in men were very light', was true only for VIII Corps up to the end of 18 July, not for the whole battle.

On 23 July First Canadian Army was activated under the Canadian Lt-Gen Sir Harry Crerar, consisting of II Canadian Corps and I (British) Corps. 7th Armoured Division and Guards Armoured Division remained in the Orne bridgehead, as there was one more big attack to make. After meeting Montgomery on 20 July, Eisenhower had issued a letter reminding him that American numbers were shortly to dominate in Normandy, 'But while we have equality in size we must go forward shoulder to shoulder, with honours and sacrifices equally shared.' Montgomery responded on 24 July with plans for attacks by

Second Army and First Canadian Army to assist First US Army's break-out, culminating in a drive to Falaise. The start of this was Operation 'Spring', a strike southwards from Verrières ridge by II Canadian Corps with 7th Armoured Division attached and Guards Armoured Division held in reserve. Operation Cobra, which depended on the heavy bombers of Eighth Air Force, was once more delayed due to weather problems, and Cobra and Spring finally took place together on 25 July. Although Spring ended in failure by nightfall, Army Group B remained uncertain which was the main Allied break-out attempt. The deciding evidence was that Cobra, and not Spring, had used heavy bombers, which the Germans now recognised as an essential part of major Allied offensives.

As Rommel had predicted on 9 July, Army Group B could not hold its line in Normandy and Operation Cobra (indirectly assisted by Operation Spring) began an American break-out that would take the Allies to Paris and the River Seine within four weeks. On 7 August, II Canadian Corps mounted a second attack against Verrières ridge in Operation 'Totalize', and this time broke through. For the British and Canadians, the next battles in Normandy would not be for Caen, but for the road to Falaise.

The price. The Commonwealth War Graves Commission cemetery at Sannerville, which contains the graves of many who died during Operation Goodwood. *(SCT)*

PART THREE

BATTLEFIELD TOURS

GENERAL TOURING INFORMATION

Normandy is a thriving holiday area, with some beautiful countryside, excellent beaches and very attractive architecture (particularly in the case of religious buildings). It was also, of course, the scene of heavy fighting in 1944, and this has had a considerable impact on the tourist industry. To make the most of your trip, especially if you intend visiting non-battlefield sites, we strongly recommend you purchase one of the general Normandy guidebooks that are commonly available. These include: *Michelin Green Guide: Normandy*; *Thomas Cook Travellers: Normandy*; *The Rough Guide to Brittany and Normandy*; *Lonely Planet: Normandy*.

TRAVEL REQUIREMENTS

First, make sure you have the proper documentation to enter France as a tourist. Citizens of European Union countries, including Great Britain, should not usually require visas, but will need to carry and show their passports. Others should check with the French Embassy in their own country before travelling. British citizens should also fill in and take Form E111 (available from main post offices), which deals with entitlement to medical treatment, and all should consider taking out comprehensive travel insurance. France is part of the Eurozone, and you should also check exchange rates before travelling.

GETTING THERE

The most direct routes from the UK to Lower Normandy are by ferry from Portsmouth to Ouistreham (near Caen), and from Portsmouth or Poole to Cherbourg. Depending on which you choose, and whether you travel by day or night, the crossing takes between four and seven hours. Alternatively, you can sail to Le Havre, Boulogne or Calais and drive the rest of the way. (Travel time from Calais to Caen is about four hours; motorway

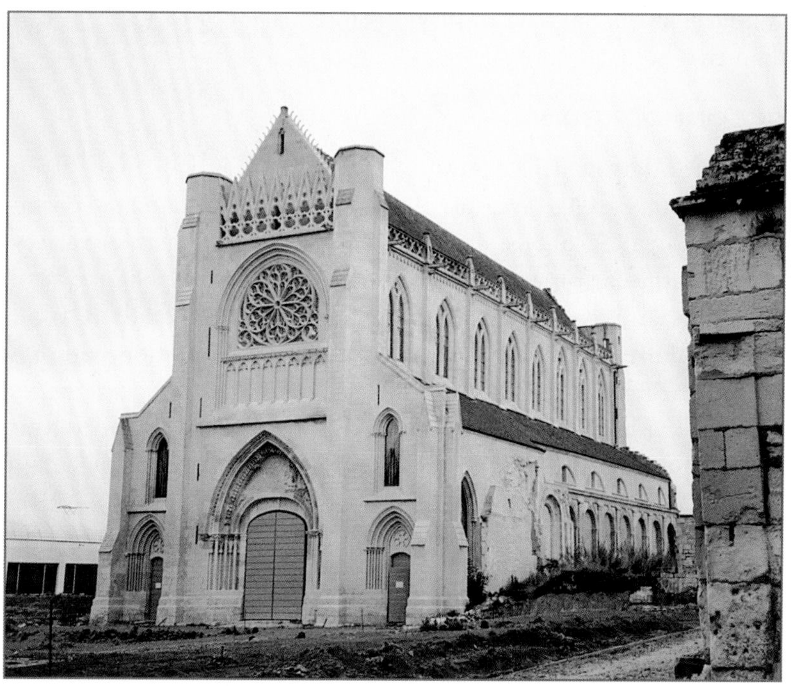

Above: September 2004. Sixty years after its near-destruction, repair work approaches completion at the Ardennes Abbey. *(SCT)*

Page 105: Cromwell tanks of 2nd Northants Yeomanry approach their start line on 18 July. Ranville church is in the background. *(IWM B7563)*

and bridge tolls may be payable depending on the exact route taken.) Another option is to use the Channel Tunnel. Whichever way you decide to travel, early booking is advised, especially during the summer months.

Although you can of course hire motor vehicles in Normandy, the majority of visitors from the UK or other EU countries will probably take their own. If you do so, you will also need to take: a full driving licence; your vehicle registration document; a certificate of motor insurance valid in France (your insurer will advise on this); spare headlight and indicator bulbs; headlight beam adjusters or tape; a warning triangle; and a sticker or number plate identifying which country the vehicle is registered in. Visitors from elsewhere should consult a motoring organisation in their home country for details of the documents and other items they will require.

Normandy's road system is well developed, although there are still a few choke points, especially around the larger towns during rush hour and in the holiday season. As a general guide, in clear conditions it is possible to drive from Cherbourg to Caen in less than two hours.

ACCOMMODATION

Accommodation in Normandy is plentiful and diverse, from cheap campsites to five-star hotels in glorious châteaux. Caen itself has over 60 hotels, catering to a range of budgets. A variety of accommodation can also be found in Bayeux, Falaise, and along the invasion coastline. Owing to the excellent road infrastructure of Lower Normandy, almost any location within a 50-km radius can be used as a base for undertaking the tours covered in this book. However, early booking is advised if you wish to travel between June and August. Useful contacts include:

French Travel Centre, 178 Piccadilly, London W1V 0AL; tel: 0870 830 2000; web: www.raileurope.co.uk
French Tourist Authority, 444 Madison Avenue, New York, NY 10022 (other offices in Chicago, Los Angeles and Miami); web: www.francetourism.com
Calvados Tourisme, Place du Canada, 14000 Caen; tel: +33 (0)2 31 86 53 30; web: www.calvados-tourisme.com
Caen Tourist Information Centre, Hôtel d'Escoville, Place St-Pierre, 14000 Caen; tel: +33 (0)2 31 27 14 14; web: www.caen.fr/tourisme

All that remains of the Colombelles steelworks today. The bases of three former factory chimneys can be seen on the right. *(SCT)*

The ruins of the Colombelles industrial area, seen after the battle. *(IWM CL 498)*

Office de Tourisme Intercommunal de Bayeux, Pont Saint-Jean, 14400 Bayeux; tel: +33 (0)2 31 51 28 28; web: www.bayeux-tourism.com
Manche Tourisme; web: www.manchetourisme.com
Maison du Tourisme de Cherbourg et du Haut-Cotentin, 2 Quai Alexandre III, 50100 Cherbourg-Octeville; tel: +33 (0)2 33 93 52 02; web: www.ot-cherbourg-cotentin.fr
Gîtes de France, La Maison des Gîtes de France et du Tourisme Vert, 59 Rue Saint-Lazare, 75 439 Paris Cedex 09; tel: +33 (0)1 49 70 75 75; web: www.gites-de-france.fr

In Normandy itself there are tourist offices in all the large towns and many of the small ones, especially along the coast.

BATTLEFIELD TOURING

Each volume in the 'Battle Zone Normandy' series contains from four to six battlefield tours. These are intended to last from a few hours to a full day apiece. Some are best undertaken using motor transport, others should be done on foot, and many involve a mixture of the two. Owing to its excellent infrastructure and relatively gentle topography, Normandy also makes a good location for a cycling holiday; indeed, some of our tours are ideally suited to this method.

Street sign, Cussy. This is one of numerous ways in which the events of 1944 are commemorated. *(SCT)*

In every case the tour author has visited the area concerned recently, so the information presented should be reasonably up to date and accurate, but land use, infrastructure and rights of way can change, sometimes at short notice. If you encounter any difficulties in following a tour, we would very much like to hear about it, so we can incorporate changes in future editions. Your comments should be sent to the publisher at the address provided at the front of this book.

To derive maximum value and enjoyment from the tours, we suggest you equip yourself with the following items:

- Appropriate maps. European road atlases can be purchased from a wide range of locations outside France. However, for navigation within Normandy, the French Institut Géographique National (IGN) produces maps at a variety of scales (www.ign.fr). The 1:100,000 series ('Top 100') is particularly useful when driving over larger distances; sheet 06 (Caen – Cherbourg) covers most of the invasion area. For pinpointing locations precisely, the current IGN 1:25,000 Série Bleue is best (extracts from this series are used for the tour maps in this book). These can be purchased in many places across Normandy. They can also be ordered in the UK from some bookshops, or from specialist dealers such as the Hereford Map Centre, 24–25 Church Street, Hereford HR1 2LR; tel: 01432 266322; web: <www.themapcentre.com>. Allow at least a fortnight's notice, although some maps may be in stock.
- Lightweight waterproof clothing and robust footwear are essential, especially for touring in the countryside.
- Take a compass, provided you know how to use one!
- A camera and spare films/memory cards.
- A notebook to record what you have photographed.
- A French dictionary and/or phrasebook. (English is widely spoken in the coastal area, but is much less common as you move inland.)

- Food and drink. Although you are never very far in Normandy from a shop, restaurant or *tabac*, many of the tours do not pass directly by such facilities. It is therefore sensible to take some light refreshment with you.
- Binoculars. Most officers and some other ranks carried binoculars in 1944. Taking a pair adds a surprising amount of verisimilitude to the touring experience.

SOME DO'S AND DON'TS

Battlefield touring can be an extremely interesting and even emotional experience, especially if you have read something about the battles beforehand. In addition, it is fair to say that residents of Normandy are used to visitors, among them battlefield tourers, and generally will do their best to help if you encounter problems. However, many of the tours in the 'Battle Zone Normandy' series are off the beaten track, and you can expect some puzzled looks from the locals, especially inland. In all cases we have tried to ensure that tours are on public land, or viewable from public rights of way. However, in the unlikely event that you are asked to leave a site, do so immediately and by the most direct route.

In addition: **Never remove 'souvenirs' from the battlefields.** Even today it is not unknown for farmers to turn up relics of the 1944 fighting. Taking these without permission may not only be illegal, but can be extremely dangerous. It also ruins the site for genuine battlefield archaeologists. Anyone returning from France should also remember customs regulations on the import of weapons and ammunition of any kind.

This memorial, erected in 1995 to commemorate the battle for Carpiquet, stands near the modern control tower on the northern edge of the airfield. *(SCT)*

Be especially careful when investigating fortifications. Some of the more frequently-visited sites are well preserved, and several of them have excellent museums. However, both along the coast and inland there are numerous positions that have been left to decay, and which carry risks for the unwary. In particular, remember that many of these places were the scenes of heavy fighting or subsequent demolitions, which may have caused severe (and sometimes invisible) structural damage. Coastal erosion has also undermined the foundations of a number of shoreline defences. Under no circumstances should underground bunkers, chambers and tunnels be entered, and care should always be taken when examining above-ground structures. If in any doubt, stay away.

Lébisey woods, looking south-east from near the Château de la Londe. In 1944 the woods were separated from Caen by over 2 km of farmland. Now they mark the northern edge of the city. *(SCT)*

Beware of hunting (shooting) areas (signposted *Chasse Gardée*). Do not enter these, even if they offer a short cut to your destination. Similarly, Normandy contains a number of restricted areas (military facilities and wildlife reserves), which should be avoided. Watch out, too, for temporary footpath closures, especially along sections of coastal cliffs.

If using a motor vehicle, keep your eyes on the road. There are many places to park, even on minor routes, and it is always better to turn round and retrace your path than to cause an accident. In rural areas avoid blocking entrances and driving along farm tracks; again, it is better to walk a few hundred metres than to cause damage and offence.

THINGS TO DO IN THE CAEN AREA

Caen lies only a short distance from the Normandy coast, with its wide sandy beaches and attractive coastal resorts. The countryside is rich and fertile, with many pretty towns and villages and some beautiful châteaux and religious buildings. Extensive details of things to see in the area west and south of Caen can be found in other volumes of 'Battle Zone Normandy', which also identify numerous military museums and other battle-related sites.

Useful Addresses

Bateau l'Hastings Boat Trips (Caen – Pegasus Bridge – Ouistreham), Quai Vendeuvre, BP 3052, 14018 Caen, Cedex 2; tel: +33 (0)2 31 34 00 00; web: www.bateau-hasting.com

Bowling du Calvados, 10-Pin Bowling Alley, 6 Rue Charles Coulomb, Mondeville; tel: +33 (0)2 31 82 53 58

La Prairie Children's Activity Centre, 11 Avenue Sorel, 14000 Caen; tel: +33 (0)2 31 85 25 16; web: www.la-prairie.com

Caen Museum of Fine Arts (Beaux-Arts Museum), le Château, 14000 Caen; tel: +33 (0)2 31 30 47 70; web: www.ville-caen.fr/mba

Museum of Normandy (Musée de Normandie), le Château; tel: +33 (0)2 31 30 47 50; web: www.ville-caen-fr/mdn

Caen Memorial Museum, Esplanade Dwight Eisenhower, BP 6261, 14066 Caen, Cedex 4; tel +33 (0)2 31 06 06 44; web: www.memorial-caen.fr

Nature Museum, Caen City Hall; tel: +33 (0)2 31 30 43 27

Parc Festyland theme park, Route de Caumont-Bretteville-sur-Odon; tel: +33 (0)2 31 75 04 04; web: www.festyland.com

Go-kart track; tel: +33 (0)2 31 83 09 53; web: www.karting-indoor-caen.com

Caen is a city of almost 200,000 people, with all the facilities that one associates with a settlement of this size, plus a large university. Although the industrial and commercial zone around the ring road is unremarkable and offers little of interest, the heart of the city is attractive and well worth a visit. Despite a few signs of wartime damage, a major post-war rebuilding programme restored parts of the old town with a considerable degree of sympathy to the original architecture and street plan. Many old buildings, including a number of churches and the splendid castle, are open to the public, and there are some interesting museums, notably the Caen Memorial 'Peace Museum' in the north-west part of the city. There are also many excellent restaurants and an extensive range of shops. Details of some of the most obvious sites of interest are given in the accompanying box, but further details

can be gained from the websites listed on pp. 108–9 or the guidebooks listed at the start of this section.

THE CAEN TOURS

This book contains four battlefield tours, covering a cross-section of the fighting for the city of Caen. An effort has been made to recognise the contribution both of British and Canadian forces, although inevitably, with a struggle on this scale, it has been impossible to provide details of every action. Also, the expansion of Caen has removed many traces of the battlefield as it was in 1944, especially on the north-eastern and eastern sides of the city, where several villages important in the fighting have been swallowed by urban sprawl or almost completely rebuilt. A few important sites are also on private property – for example the hamlet of Galmanche, scene of fierce fighting between elements of 59th (Staffordshire) Division and II/25th SS Panzergrenadier Regiment on 8–9 July. Nevertheless, much of the battlefield is remarkably unchanged. By using this book, perhaps with the aid of further research, you could expand the tours into new areas – for example, the Verrières Ridge south of Caen, or the Sannerville–Troarn area on the eastern side of the Goodwood battlefield.

The Canadian cemetery at Bény-Reviers, with the grave of one of the Regina Rifles' officers killed during the attack on the Ardennes Abbey on 8 July in the foreground. *(Jonathan Falconer)*

Many tourers will want to visit the cemeteries containing the graves of those killed during the fighting described in this book. Most of the British and Canadian soldiers who died during the battle for Caen were buried at one of the following Commonwealth War Graves Commission (CWGC) cemeteries: Banneville-Sannerville (next to the N175 just west of Sannerville); Cambes-en-Plaine (near the D7 road north of Caen); Douvres-la-Délivrande (by the D7 on the southern edge of Douvres); Ranville (near Pegasus Bridge on the east side of the River Orne); and Bény-Reviers (the Canadian cemetery, near the D170 half-way between Courseulles-sur-Mer and

Caen). Further details can be found on the CWGC website, www.cwgc.org

Although the tour maps provide extensive details of the 'Windsor', 'Charnwood' and 'Goodwood' battlefields, for complete coverage of the battle area, and of Caen itself, you will find it helpful to purchase the IGN 1:25000-scale Série Bleue map sheet 1612 OT 'Caen-Ouistreham'.

TOUR A

OPERATION 'WINDSOR'

OBJECTIVE: This tour covers 8th Canadian Infantry Brigade's attempt to capture Carpiquet village and airfield from elements of 12th SS Panzer Division *Hitlerjugend* on 4 July.

View north along the D147a, with the woods at Point 82 on the right. The track to Stand A1 is visible below the wooded area. *(SCT)*

DURATION/SUITABILITY: The tour lasts 2–3 hours, and could precede Tour B to make a full day. The total distance is about 9 km. The roads are fairly busy, but the tour can be undertaken by bicycle. For tourers with mobility difficulties, all stands are visible from a vehicle.

To BAYEUX
St-Germain-la-Blanche-Herbe
Carpiquet
Bretteville-sur-Odon
St-Manvieu-Norrey
Aérodrome de Caen-Carpiquet
Marcelet
Franqueville
Beaulieu
la Baulue
Venoix
N13
N175
D9
D220
D147a
N413
A1
A2
A3
A4
A5
1 Royal Winnipeg Rifles, 4 July
2 Le Régiment de la Chaudière, 4 July
3 North Shore (New Brunswick) Regiment, 4 July
4 Queen's Own Rifles of Canada, 4 July
5 3/26th and elements 1/26th SS Panzergrenadiers
6 HQ I/26th SS Panzergrenadiers, elements 1/26th, 2/26th, 4/26th SS Panzergrenadiers
7 Five Panzer IVs, 9th/12th SS Panzers
8 2/12th SS Flak
9 German counter-attacks, 5 July
a Site of north hangars
b Site of south hangars
0
1
2

Stand A1: Point 82

DIRECTIONS: Leave the Caen ring road on the N175, heading for Villers-Bocage. Exit at the first junction and drive north along the D147a, signposted to St-Manvieu. Note the dominating position of the airfield, which is on the high ground before you. After 1 km, turn right onto an unsurfaced track. Drive slowly, or park your vehicle and walk to Stand A1. In either case, follow the track uphill and stop when you reach the woods to your left. You are now about 800 metres from the wartime site of the airfield's southern hangars (which no longer exist), and 2 km from the buildings at the eastern end of the runway. The woods here are those to which the Royal Winnipeg Rifles retreated after the battalion's unsuccessful attempt to capture the hangars on the morning of 4 July.

THE ACTION: Operation Windsor began at 0500 hours, with a thunderous bombardment by massed artillery and naval guns. The assault battalions of 8th Canadian Infantry Brigade advanced behind a rolling barrage 365 metres deep and 2.5 km wide. Most of the troops headed for Carpiquet village, but the Royal Winnipeg Rifles (attached from 7th Brigade) thrust from Marcelet towards the hangars on the south edge of the airfield. This objective was important, since without it the planned attack by the Queen's Own Rifles of Canada (8th Brigade's reserve battalion) against the eastern end of the airfield could not take place. The Winnipegs were accompanied by a troop of 17-pounder M10 tank destroyers from 62nd Anti-Tank Regiment, RA, plus several 'Crocodile' flame-throwing tanks. A squadron of the Fort Garry Horse (Sherman tanks) also provided fire support from near the start line.

Opposition to the Winnipegs was considerable. Their objective was defended by the headquarters of I/26th SS Panzergrenadiers, plus most of the battalion's 1st, 2nd and 4th Companies – a total of at least 250 men, protected by strong underground shelters. Five Panzer IVs from 9/12th SS Panzer Regiment were located 1 km further east, with at least one company of Panthers in reserve in Bretteville-sur-Odon. In addition, II/1st SS Panzergrenadiers (from 1st SS Panzer Division) held the area around Verson and les Jumeaux, from which they could bring fire to bear against the high ground further north. Powerful artillery assets, including the guns of 12th SS and 1st SS Panzer Divisions and several rocket-launcher

(*Nebelwerfer*) battalions, were also available. Thanks to intercepted Canadian radio traffic, which gave warning of the impending attack, these units were ready to provide immediate fire support. They had also bombarded the Winnipegs as they entered Marcelet on 3 July, and maintained a steady fire against the Canadian assembly area during the night before the assault.

Stand A1, looking east. The Winnipegs attacked from left to right towards the small mound in the centre-right, which marks the approximate location of the southern hangars. The red-roofed buildings at the end of the runway can be seen at top left in the wartime photo on p. 124. *(SCT)*

Despite the casualties, disruption and lack of sleep caused by the German shelling, the Winnipegs' advance initially proceeded satisfactorily, and the leading companies pushed through a haze of smoke and dust without meeting much opposition. However, while they were still some distance from the hangars, the German bombardment intensified, inflicting numerous losses. German machine guns also opened fire, and the Winnipegs began to lose momentum. Nevertheless, at 0756 hours 8th Brigade's war diary recorded that the hangars had been reached, and instructions were issued for the Queen's Own Rifles to prepare to launch its own attack towards the airfield control buildings and barracks.

In fact, the Winnipegs' position was precarious. Those men who had arrived at the hangars were exhausted and their units had lost their cohesion. None of their supporting armour appears to have reached the objective, and when a troop of the Fort Garry Horse was finally urged forward, two tanks were quickly knocked out (probably by the Panzer IVs at the eastern end of the airfield) and the others retired. Faced with fanatical opposition from the surviving SS defenders, after several hours of close-quarters fighting Lt-Col J.M. Meldram ordered a retreat. At 1330 hours the Winnipegs pulled back to the copse where you are standing, where Meldram hoped to regroup for another attempt on the hangars.

At about 1600 hours the Canadians renewed their attack, but again met heavy resistance from their right flank and front. The leading companies reached the objective, but saw tanks massing to the east for a counter-attack. I Corps' artillery dispersed the panzers on several occasions, but each time they rallied. Faced with the danger of being overrun, during the evening the Winnipegs retired to a position near Marcelet, where they dug in. The battalion's casualties on 4 July were 132 men, including 40 killed. However, owing to the loss of Carpiquet village, the survivors of I/26th SS Panzergrenadiers also retreated overnight to the eastern end of the airfield. As a result, the hangars were left in no-man's-land, where they remained until 9 July, when they were occupied by Le Régiment de la Chaudière.

Stand A2: 8th Brigade's start line

DIRECTIONS: Rejoin your vehicle and continue north on the D147a. There is a new by-pass around Marcelet, not shown on the current IGN map, which joins the D9 just west of the village. Turn right onto the D9 and continue to the signposts shown in the photo overleaf. Turn right here and pull over. Then walk back to the junction, cross the D9 and proceed 100 metres along the track on the other side. This was the start line for 8th Brigade's attack, with Le Régiment de la Chaudière jumping off from where you are now standing, and the North Shore (New Brunswick) Regiment beginning its assault from a point about 1 km further north, near the railway line and modern factory buildings.

THE SITE: From Stand A2, look east to the outskirts of Carpiquet village, which was defended on 4 July by 3/26th SS Panzergrenadiers and a platoon from 1st Company, many of them occupying a series of abandoned anti-aircraft positions in the fields in front of you. There were also two 75-mm infantry guns from 4th (Heavy Weapons) Company on the eastern edge of

Carpiquet, and powerful artillery support was available. Given I/26th SS Panzergrenadiers' earlier losses, the estimated strength of the defenders was around 200 men. A battery of 88-mm flak guns was positioned near St-Germain-la-Blanche-Herbe, covering the open ground and railway crossings east of Carpiquet.

Looking east along the D9, with the modern airport control tower in the centre. Turn right towards the 'Restaurant les 3 Clubs' for Stand A3. *(SCT)*

THE ACTION: Despite some disruption caused by harassing artillery fire, fog and the problems of navigating through the wheat fields that covered this area in 1944, 8th Brigade's assault battalions moved up to their start line before dawn, and were ready for the attack by 0500 hours. Each battalion deployed two companies forward and two behind, supported by around 40 Shermans of the Fort Garry Horse and various specialised vehicles, including flail tanks, AVREs and Crocodiles. Machine-gun support was provided by the 1st Cameron Highlanders of Ottawa, firing over the troops' heads as they advanced.

At H-Hour the barrage started, and after about 10 minutes the Canadians set off through almost impenetrable clouds of dust and smoke. These provided cover against direct fire, but also led to intermingling of units and some loss of direction. Considerable casualties were inflicted by the German counter-bombardment, which began as the attack was launched. Nevertheless, at 0632 hours elements of the North Shore Regiment reported that they were at edge of the village, and soon afterwards the rest of the battalion entered Carpiquet.

Major Clint Gammon, commanding the North Shores' D Company, described the assault:

'All the way across we flushed out or killed enemy who had stayed in the slit trenches until the last minute. At last we came within 200 yards of the village and for some reason or other the enemy fire slackened considerably... I went to the troop leader of the tanks and told him to cut off his fire as we were forming up to assault the village. He said okay and the minute I walked around in front of the tank somebody fired the big gun, which resulted in my being knocked out. I remember how quiet everything was. I thought I was dead because there was no noise, no fire, no grain burning. Everything was so peaceful.'

Source: Will Bird, *North Shore (New Brunswick) Regiment*, p. 267.

View north across the D9 (the track leads to Stand A2), looking along the start line for 8th Brigade's attack. The Canadians suffered heavy losses here at the start of their assault. *(SCT)*

By 0716 hours the North Shores' A and D Companies were inside the village, where they found very few Germans. However, although Carpiquet was cleared within an hour, by the time the Canadians dug in along its eastern edge intense mortar and artillery fire was falling throughout the village. This continued unremittingly, inflicting further losses on the North Shores, 46 of whom were killed (with 86 wounded) by the day's end. Nevertheless, the battalion held firm, directing mortar and artillery fire against the German positions further to the east. As their war diary remarked, after such a hard-won success there could be 'no thought of withdrawal.'

Sturmmann **(Lance-Corporal) Karl-Heinz Wambach of 3/26th SS Panzergrenadiers was among the defenders:**

'Immediately after the barrage, the leading tanks rolled towards us, accompanied by infantry. 3rd Company, already badly weakened, could withstand the enemy material superiority for only a short time. Firing a green flare [to call down fire support] caused an enemy tank to roll towards my foxhole, do a full turn and cover me with dirt up to my chest. The fire support never came. I managed to free my arms. Only scattered fire came from the positions of 3rd Company. Enemy tanks were sitting everywhere... Three of them were on fire and, above the dug-up edge of my foxhole, I could see tanks advancing in the direction of the airfield. From a clump of trees an "88" fired on the hesitant enemy. This had to be about 11 a.m. and I was still unable to free my legs and hips. Suddenly a voice yelled behind me, 'SS bastard, hands up!' Two Canadians pulled me from my prison, tied my hands and then hit me in the face with full force.'

Source: Hubert Meyer, *The History of the 12. SS-Panzerdivision Hitlerjugend*, p. 136.

Stand A3: The Aéro-club

DIRECTIONS: Rejoin your vehicle and follow the minor road to the Aéro-club. Look east across the runway for a good view of the red-roofed hangars that mark the site of the wartime control buildings and barracks (now an industrial zone). Then face north-east towards the modern terminal and control tower. In July 1944 four double-width hangars lined the road to the right of these structures, although all were badly damaged in the battle and subsequently demolished.

THE SITE: This stand provides you with an excellent position from which to see a large part of the battlefield, and to orientate

yourself to 8th Brigade's attacks, as well as to the objective of the Queen's Own Rifles of Canada at the end of the runway.

The modern airport buildings, seen from the Aéro-club. The large building visible through the haze to the right is the hospital in northern Caen. It can be seen from many directions, and is useful for orientation purposes. *(SCT)*

THE ACTION: Attacking along the line of the D9, Le Régiment de la Chaudière suffered numerous casualties to German artillery, but made good progress. Its B and D Companies soon reached the edge of Carpiquet, and A and C Companies then passed through to clear the southern part of the village. By 1100 hours the battalion had overrun the northern hangars, before digging in under heavy fire to protect its gains. Machine-gun detachments from the Cameron Highlanders of Ottawa also moved forward, reinforcing 8th Brigade's defences throughout Carpiquet.

Le Régiment de la Chaudière's war diary emphasised the strength of the German positions along the airfield's northern perimeter:

'The enemy was solidly organised. His infantry positions consisted of almost perfectly camouflaged trenches which were well protected against fire. The Germans also had many machine-gun nests and concrete emplacements, the reinforced walls of which were at least six feet thick with roofs supported by solid pieces of steel. We needed the support of the Crocodiles [flame-thrower tanks] to clear

Carpiquet airfield in 1944, looking south-east, with the northern hangars on the right. Le Régiment de la Chaudière cleared the area in the foreground, including a number of aircraft dispersal sites and the hangars themselves. *(IWM CL609)*

> these almost impregnable positions... [Our] battalion headquarters was established in a German dugout. This dugout was very solid but attracted almost constant enemy fire. Throughout the afternoon and night the Germans rained a veritable deluge of artillery shells and mortar bombs onto our positions. We lost many men, killed and wounded.'
>
> *Source:* War Diary, Le Régiment de la Chaudière, 4 July, UK National Archives.

Despite the successes achieved by 8th Brigade, the Winnipegs' inability to capture their objectives caused phase two of Operation Windsor – the attack on the airfield control buildings – to be postponed at 1400 hours, and then cancelled. Consequently, although the soldiers of the Queen's Own Rifles advanced as far as the western edge of Carpiquet, they ended their day by digging in to help defend the village against counter-attacks. Their casualties on 4 July amounted to 4 killed and 22 wounded; Le Régiment de la Chaudière lost 57 men, 16 of whom were killed.

Stand A4: The Airport Terminal

DIRECTIONS: Return to the D9 and turn right. After 1.5 km turn right again, into the modern airport. Follow the road towards the terminal building to view the *Luftwaffe* accommodation bunker shown in the photo, and then drive a short distance towards the control tower to examine the Canadian memorial (*see p. 111*).

A *Luftwaffe* accommodation bunker at Carpiquet, a few metres from the modern terminal building. The photo is taken looking west, with the fields through which Le Régiment de la Chaudière attacked on the right. *(SCT)*

THE SITE: Other than the large concrete bunker and memorial, there is little to see here. However, it is worth pausing to compare the aerial photo opposite with the current layout of the airport buildings, and to get a different view of the battlefield.

Stand A5: Carpiquet village

DIRECTIONS: Rejoin the D9, heading east into Carpiquet. A short distance into the village, pull over on the right, opposite the Canadian memorial (next to the flagpoles). Cross the road and walk 100 metres east to see a second monument, this time to the North Shore Regiment.

THE SITE: Although Carpiquet was substantially rebuilt after the war, parts of the village – especially near the church – are original. It is particularly worth visiting the farm at the north-western edge of Carpiquet to see the kind of robust stone-built structure that existed here in 1944.

This monument beside the D9 in Carpiquet bears a plaque to the Fort Garry Horse, which helped capture the village. *(SCT)*

THE ACTION: Following the loss of Carpiquet, the Germans made several attempts to retake it. These involved elements of 1st SS Panzer Division, assisted by some tanks from the *Hitlerjugend*. The most serious counter-attack occurred at about 0230 hours on 5 July, when I/1st SS Panzergrenadiers stormed across the railway embankment at the north-eastern edge of Carpiquet, preceded by an intense bombardment that set light to almost every building in the village. However, the North Shore and Cameron Highlanders' machine guns beat off the attack, inflicting severe casualties in the process (I/1st SS Panzergrenadiers lost 116 men). An attempt by III/1st SS Panzergrenadiers to break into the south-eastern part of the village later the same morning was more successful, and a company of Le Régiment de la Chaudière was briefly overrun before the Germans were driven out. However, following the repulse of this counter-attack, the Germans generally restricted themselves to pounding Carpiquet with artillery and mortar fire.

This made life extremely unpleasant for the Canadians, who were predictably delighted when Operation Charnwood facilitated their departure from the devastated village on 9 July.

TO CONCLUDE THE TOUR: To return to Caen, continue along the D9, heading straight ahead at the crossroads in eastern Carpiquet.

TO CONTINUE WITH TOUR B: Turn left onto the D14 at the crossroads in eastern Carpiquet. Continue north across the railway (where I/1st SS Panzergrenadiers counter-attacked on 5 July) and join the N13 heading west, towards Bayeux. Then follow the directions to Stand B1 provided below.

TOUR B

OPERATION 'CHARNWOOD'

OBJECTIVE: This tour examines the first day of I Corps' offensive to capture Caen, focusing on 3rd Canadian Division's assault north-west of the city.

DURATION/SUITABILITY: The tour lasts half a day, and can be combined with Tour A to make a full day. The total distance is 7.5 km, mostly along moderately busy roads. It is suitable for cyclists and those with mobility difficulties.

Stand B1: Point 59

DIRECTIONS: Leave Caen on the N13, signposted to Bayeux and Cherbourg. After 2.5 km exit onto the D83c (the old main road, running parallel with the modern N13), and turn right after 1 km onto the D170. Drive through Rots and Rosel to Cairon. At Cairon turn right onto the D22, heading back towards Caen. Drive through Cairon le Vieux and leave the village at its south-eastern edge. A high bank on your left obscures visibility to the north, but you can easily see into the valley on your right. This feature provided cover for Canadian troops preparing to attack Gruchy, 1 km to the

0 1 2
Kilometres
1 Stormont, Dundas and Glengarry Highlanders
2 Highland Light Infantry of Canad
3 Elements 59th (Staffordshire) Di
4 North Nova Scotia Highlanders
5 1st Canadian Scottish
6 Regina Rifle Regiment
7 Elements II/25th SS Panzergrena
8 11/25th SS Panzergrenadiers
9 10/25th SS Panzergrenadiers
10 9/25th SS Panzergrenadiers
11 14/25th SS Panzergrenadiers
12 16/25th SS Panzergrenadiers
13 HQ 25th SS Panzergrenadiers
14 3/12th SS Panzers, afternoon 8 J
Base map: IGN 1612OT
To BAYEUX
Cairon
Villons-les-Buissons
les Buissons
Cairon le Vieux
Rosel
Buron
Gruchy
Hameau de St-Louet
Authie
Cussy
St-Contest
Franqueville
Ardennes
St-Germain-la-Blanche-Herbe
Carpiquet

south, on 8 July. Drive uphill until you reach level ground, and park on the right where two large farm tracks meet the road.

THE SITE: You are now standing on the axis of 9th Canadian Infantry Brigade's attack, about 300 metres from the start line near Cairon le Vieux. Buron is directly in front of you, with Gruchy a few hundred metres further south. These two villages were 9th Brigade's initial objectives on 8 July. Buron has expanded considerably in recent years, and its western edge is now much closer to Point 59 than it was in 1944. By comparison, Gruchy has changed relatively little. The same is true of most of the fields around you, which are as open and devoid of cover as they were 60 years ago.

View from near Stand B1, looking north-west towards the Glens' start line at Cairon le Vieux, hidden in the dead ground in the middle distance. *(SCT)*

THE ACTION: Operation Charnwood involved all three of I Corps' divisions, attacking almost simultaneously to capture the northern part of Caen. In 3rd Canadian Division's sector the initial assault was carried out by 9th Infantry Brigade, which was responsible for taking the villages of Buron, Gruchy, Authie and Franqueville, plus the Château de St. Louet (Hameau de St-Louet on modern maps). It was to be followed by 7th Infantry Brigade, with objectives at Cussy and Ardennes Abbey. Powerful artillery support was available for the attack, which followed an intense air bombardment of the northern outskirts of Caen on 7 July. Elements of the Canadian 2nd Armoured Brigade also assisted the attack.

Opposing the Canadians was 12th SS Panzer Division, whose 25th SS Panzergrenadier Regiment held a series of strongpoints from Franqueville in the west to the fields south of Cambes (in 59th Division's sector) in the east. The regiment was supported by a handful of Panzer IVs, which were stationed in Buron and Gruchy. A counter-attack force of 17 Panthers from 3/12th SS Panzers was located near Ardennes Abbey, which was also the headquarters of 25th SS Panzergrenadiers and III/12th SS Panzer Artillery. In clear conditions, observers in the towers of the abbey could see the entire battlefield, and call down fire on the Allied troops as they advanced.

Highland Light Infantry officers are briefed on the forthcoming attack, 8 July. Many of the men in this photograph were killed or wounded later the same day. *(NAC PA-116520)*

9th Infantry Brigade's two assault battalions moved into their assembly areas during the night of 7–8 July. The Highland Light Infantry of Canada (HLI) formed up near le Vey, a few hundred metres east of Cairon, while the Stormont, Dundas and Glengarry Highlanders (the Glens) concentrated at Cairon le Vieux. The North Nova Scotia Highlanders, who were to capture Authie after Buron was secured by the HLI, assembled in les Buissons. Each assault battalion was reinforced by a squadron of 15 Sherman tanks from

27th Armoured Regiment (The Sherbrooke Fusiliers), along with detachments of towed and self-propelled anti-tank guns, engineers and signallers. At about 0630 hours the troops were notified that the attack would begin 60 minutes later, and they set off towards their start line. Meanwhile, artillery pounded Buron and Gruchy in an attempt to neutralise their defences before the assault.

At 0730 hours the Canadians began their attack through thick clouds of smoke and dust, accompanied by the deafening noise of the bombardment. On the right, the HLI's D Company advanced towards Buron alongside the D22, together with four Shermans from No. 1 Troop, A Squadron, The Sherbrooke Fusiliers. B Company and No. 2 Troop approached Buron from the north, on the east side of the D220. Meanwhile, south of the D22 the Glens also moved forward, A and B Companies leading, supported by the tanks of the Sherbrooke Fusiliers' B Squadron.

At first the Glens' assault went well, and at 0745 hours its headquarters reported that the assault companies had reached the enemy outpost line without encountering any opposition. A few minutes later, however, German mortars, artillery and machine guns opened fire. Despite this, A and B Companies pressed on towards Gruchy, and at 0812 hours German soldiers were observed fleeing from the far side of the village. To cut off their escape route and to prepare the ground for the Glens' intended exploitation to the Château de St. Louet, two troops of tanks moved south of Gruchy. Here they became involved in close-quarters combat against elements of 25th SS Panzergrenadiers' 14th (anti-aircraft) Company.

The intensity of the fighting is illustrated by this account from No. 1 Troop, B Squadron, The Sherbrooke Fusiliers:

'The troop put down considerable co-axial [machine-gun] fire on the enemy weapon pits in the field between Gruchy and the Château [de St. Louet]. Lieutenant Foster fired at a 20-mm anti-aircraft gun in this field and after wounding the gunner and smashing the power traverse he advanced and drove his tank into the gun. Sergeant Taylor came to within 50 yards and covered him. At this moment a German in one of the numerous foxholes surrounding the gun, threw a grenade at the turret and came extremely near to killing Lieutenant Foster. A pistol duel resulted and the man was killed. Lieutenant Foster then continued on and dumped grenades into most of the foxholes. Meanwhile Sergeant

> Taylor killed one man who tried to crawl away, and later a German PIAT [*sic*] penetrated his tank. Luckily only the ration boxes were damaged.'
>
> *Source:* Appendix B1, Sherbrooke Fusiliers' War Diary, UK National Archives.

Heavy fighting continued in and around Gruchy for over an hour. Particularly tough resistance was met in the fields between Gruchy and Buron, where 9/25th SS Panzergrenadiers were dug in. However, an improvised attack by 16 Bren Gun carriers from B Squadron, 7th Reconnaissance Regiment (which was nearby) helped the Glens' A Company and supporting armour overcome this opposition, and about 60 Germans were killed or captured. At 0938 hours the Glens reported that they had taken Gruchy, and were preparing to attack the Château de St. Louet. However, owing to the difficulties involved in securing Buron (discussed at the next three stands), their assault did not actually begin until mid-afternoon. Until then, the Glens had to endure frequent and accurate shelling of their positions, which added to the heavy losses they had already suffered in clearing their initial objective.

Stand B2: Buron – the anti-tank ditch

DIRECTIONS: Continue along the D22 into Buron. At the traffic lights in the centre of the village, turn left onto the D220, signposted to Villons-les-Buissons and Mathieu. About 200 metres beyond the edge of Buron you will see an electricity pylon to the right of the road. Park here and walk 100 metres east along the farm track.

THE SITE: From here you have excellent views over the fields over which the HLI advanced to Buron. In 1944 an anti-tank ditch 3.5 metres wide and 4.5 metres deep zig-zagged its way from west to east across the D220, slightly north of where you are now standing (there was a similar anti-tank ditch near the D22 north-west of Buron). Look east to see the village of St-Contest, easily identifiable by its distinctive telecommunications tower, and the hamlet of Galmanche. These locations were the scene of intense fighting on 8 July, involving elements of 59th Division. German resistance at Galmanche was especially tenacious, and the British infantry crossing the fields west of the hamlet suffered heavily from flanking fire before they reached St-Contest.

THE ACTION: After losing three of its accompanying Shermans to anti-tank mines, the HLI's D Company advanced to within a few hundred metres of the western edge of Buron. Simultaneously, B Company and its attached troop of tanks approached from the north. Up to this point, little opposition had been encountered. However, when the leading infantry reached the anti-tank ditch across the D220, they came under a withering fire from German machine guns, mortars and pre-registered artillery, which caused numerous casualties.

Stand B2, looking west. The 1944 anti-tank ditch ran broadly parallel with the track shown here, on its right-hand (northern) side. *(SCT)*

The HLI's war diary described the struggle to penetrate Buron's defences:

'The forward edge of the village was strongly held by a ring of defensive positions, most of which contained machine guns. These brought down continuous and devastating fire on our troops and it was almost impossible to advance through. Many times our troops were pinned to the ground by it, only to get up and go on as soon as it let up...

D Company under Major J.R. Anderson was the first company into the village [at about 0820 hours]... It had to smash its way through alone and clean out all the trenches that comprised the defensive system. It suffered heavy casualties doing this and progressed on to the orchard on the right forward side of the village with only half a company...

Meanwhile, B Company was encountering heavy opposition... [from] a strong reinforced company [10/25th SS Panzergrenadiers] equipped with at least double the usual number of automatic weapons. Tanks were called for but were out of communication. When contact was finally made the tanks feared to move forward because of the minefields. It was some time before they could be told that the left flank was free.

With the support of the tanks B Company was able to break its way through the defensive ring and proceed to clean up the enemy machine-gun posts one by one. These posts were very well dug in and it was necessary to approach the pit to the very edge before the enemy guns in them could be silenced.'

Source: HLI War Diary, 8 July, UK National Archives.

After losing approximately half its personnel and all four of its supporting tanks, B Company finally broke into Buron, where it joined D Company in attacking the surviving elements of the garrison. By 1000 hours the HLI's C and A Companies also entered the village, followed by Lt-Col F.M. Griffiths' command group and the carriers, anti-tank guns and mortars of the Support Company.

Stand B3: Buron village centre

DIRECTIONS: Return to your car and drive back into Buron. Go straight on (towards Authie) at the traffic lights and after 100 metres park on the left, by the village square. Here you will find two memorials, one to the HLI and the other to the Sherbrooke Fusiliers. After viewing these, spend a few minutes walking around this part of the village, which contains several old buildings constructed of robust Norman stone. In 1944 there were half a dozen orchards in and around Buron, remnants of which can still be seen.

THE ACTION: Despite the loss of their main defensive positions, the SS troops in Buron refused to give up the struggle. III/25th SS Panzergrenadiers' command post was located in the village, and its commander, *Hauptmann* (Captain) Fritz Steger, who was still in radio contact with regimental headquarters in the Ardennes Abbey, appears to have hoped that a counter-attack might restore the front line. Consequently, the Germans

continued fighting determinedly from the buildings, gardens and orchards throughout Buron, inflicting further heavy casualties on the HLI as they sought to consolidate their hold on the village.

Stand B3, with the Sherbrooke Fusiliers' memorial *right* and the Highland Light Infantry of Canada plaque *left*. *(SCT)*

By about 1430 hours the Canadians had mopped up most of the pockets of resistance, but found themselves exposed to heavy shelling for much of the rest of the day. The cost to the HLI was appalling. Altogether, the battalion lost 62 men killed and 200 wounded on 8 July, among them Lt-Col Griffiths and almost all the rifle company officers and senior NCOs. The Sherbrooke Fusiliers' A Squadron was reduced to less than half a dozen tanks by early afternoon. German losses are unknown, although they amounted to at least 100 officers and men. *Hauptmann* Steger, was captured after being seriously wounded. Several dozen of his soldiers, however, managed to remain undetected amidst the ruins of the village. Later that night they slipped away, rejoining their shattered regiment as it retreated through Caen on 9 July.

Stand B4: 'The 80-metre contour line'

DIRECTIONS: Follow the D220 to the southern edge of Buron and park in the housing estate on your right. Then walk a few metres further south until you can see across the fields towards Cussy, 1.5 km to the south-east.

A Sherbrooke Fusiliers Sherman passes through Buron, scene of very heavy fighting on 8 July. *(NAC PA-129034)*

THE SITE: As the map on p. 45 shows, in 1944 Buron was believed to lie on relatively high ground, with a distinctive kidney-shaped 80-metre contour line immediately south of the village. This feature was an important objective for 9th Brigade's attack, since its possession appeared to offer protection for the Nova Scotias' advance to Authie, as well as the assembly of 7th Canadian Infantry Brigade before its assault on Cussy and Ardennes Abbey. In fact, the wartime map was inaccurate. Not only is there no hilltop here, but the terrain actually rises to the east, with its highest point in St-Contest. Consequently, any troops pushing beyond Buron would find themselves in the middle of an open field, exposed to flanking fire from the east and vulnerable to counter-attacks from the direction of Caen.

THE ACTION: Following the Canadians' entry into Buron, Brigadier D.G. Cunningham, of 9th Infantry Brigade, was keen to secure the 80-metre contour as quickly as possible. At 1302 hours

he ordered the HLI to occupy the (non-existent) feature, but given the problems involved in overcoming resistance in the village itself this proved impossible. However, at about 1500 hours four tanks from the Sherbrooke Fusiliers' A Squadron managed to get onto the high ground near St-Contest. Simultaneously, the HLI deployed its own 6-pounder anti-tank guns to cover the approaches to Buron from the south-east. These were reinforced by eight 17-pounder M10 tank destroyers from the British 62nd Anti-Tank Regiment, which moved through the rubble-strewn streets of Buron to positions along the southern edge of the village.

The value of these measures was shown in the late afternoon, when German tanks attacked from the south-east. About a dozen were involved, mostly Panthers from 3/12th SS Panzers, although a few Panzer IVs joined in. A battalion of infantry in armoured half-tracks was supposed to support the attack, but failed to arrive at the assigned rendezvous. The German tanks therefore moved forward alone, skirting around Cussy before advancing towards Buron. However, as they approached the village, they came under a hail of anti-tank fire, which destroyed five Panthers and three Panzer IVs. The surviving tanks withdrew, leaving the remnants of III/25th SS Panzergrenadiers to their fate. Six of the British M10s were knocked out, although like most of the Sherbrooke Fusiliers' tanks, the majority of the damaged vehicles were later recovered.

Stand B5: Authie

DIRECTIONS: Return to your car and drive 750 metres to Authie, going straight ahead at the crossroads with the D126 north of the village. Turn right in the village centre, and park by the monument to the North Nova Scotia Highlanders, who fought a costly battle here on 7 June before finally liberating the village a month later.

THE ACTION: Although the Nova Scotias were ordered forward from les Buissons just after the first Canadian troops entered Buron, they were held up by artillery and mortar fire near Buron, and did not reach it until about 1100 hours. They then became involved in mopping up III/25th SS Panzergrenadiers, and were heavily shelled again when they reached their jumping-off position on the south side of the village. Numerous casualties were sustained (the battalion lost 201 men altogether), and the attack on Authie was severely delayed.

The disruptive effects of the German bombardment are described in the Nova Scotias' war diary:

'Major E.S. Gray, commander of A Company, was the first officer casualty of the day… Shortly after this, Major C.F. Kennedy, commanding D Company lost his right arm and passed over command to Captain S. Byrd who was also seriously wounded shortly after and lived only a few hours. It has since come to light that Major Kennedy commanded the Company for two hours with his right arm hanging by a small shred of skin which he had cut off by one of his section commanders. Captain S.V. Matson, commanding Support Company used his initiative by quickly taking over command of D Company. The battalion was then ready to move forward to its objective.'

Source: North Nova Scotia Regiment War Diary, 8 July, UK National Archives.

Canadian soldiers examine a knocked out Panther of 1/12th SS Panzers near Authie, 9 July. *(NAC PA-11467)*

At 1500 hours the Nova Scotias attacked, reaching the first houses in Authie seven minutes later. Little opposition was encountered, and the battalion set about consolidating its gains. C Company also sent patrols forward to Franqueville, which was occupied by mid-evening and secured the following day.

Stand B6: Hameau de St-Louet

DIRECTIONS: Exit Authie to the west and drive about 700 metres until you reach a patch of woodland (near the position of the original château) on your right. Turn right (north) onto a farm track where the road bends hard left, and park about 100 metres further on, at a point where you can see Gruchy in front of you.

Gruchy (*right*) and the fields to the west, seen from Stand B6. *(SCT)*

THE ACTION: On 8 July the track where you are now standing was the axis for the Glens' attack on the Château de St. Louet, which began just before 1500 hours. C and D Companies carried out the assault, assisted by six tanks from the Sherbrooke Fusiliers' B Squadron. Resistance was sporadic and ineffectual, and at 1558 hours the château was reported cleared. According to 9th Brigade's signals log, the Glens took 22 prisoners, all 17- and 18-year-olds from 16/25th SS Panzergrenadiers.

Stand B7: Ardennes Abbey

DIRECTIONS: Return to Authie and leave the village to the east, driving along the D220c towards Cussy and Caen. On 8 July this road was the axis of attack for 7th Canadian Infantry Brigade, with

the 1st Canadian Scottish Regiment advancing along and to the left of the road and the Regina Rifle Regiment on the right. Continue past Cussy and note the buildings of Ardennes Abbey on your right. Turn right just before the abbey and continue 250 metres until you reach the entrance.

THE ACTION: After spending the night at Cairon, 7th Canadian Infantry Brigade moved to its forward assembly area near Gruchy in the late morning of 8 July. Here it came under heavy artillery and mortar fire, although this caused relatively few losses. Following the capture of Authie, the assault battalions then moved to their start line on both sides of the village, reaching the jumping-off positions between 1730 and 1830 hours.

Although the sources are contradictory and timings uncertain, 1st Canadian Scottish appears to have begun its attack first. Led by A and C Companies, the battalion overran an 88-mm gun position a few hundred metres west of Cussy, where A Company consolidated. B Company then moved up along the D220c, while C Company entered the village and began clearing it of opposition. Despite heavy shelling and German tank movement on both flanks, which caused considerable concern and some casualties, by 2300 hours Cussy was secured. About 30 prisoners were taken here, mostly from 1st Battery, 12th SS Flak Battalion. The Canadian Scottish lost 122 men, including at least 34 killed.

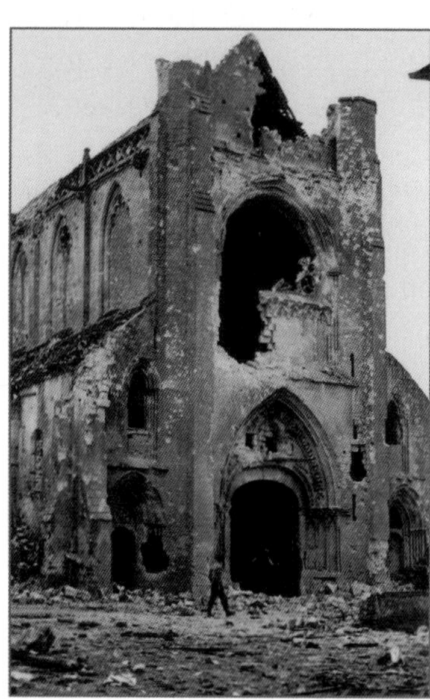

The ruins of Ardennes Abbey, photographed on 24 July 1944. *(IWM B7893)*

Meanwhile, the Regina Rifles launched their assault on Ardennes Abbey, which was fiercely defended by a mix of troops from various SS units. Most of the Canadians' tank support (from 1st Hussars) was knocked out before the attack began, and although B Company captured a defended position half-way between its start line and the final objective, the attackers suffered dreadful casualties (B Company lost some 61 men; C Company, 85). Nevertheless, by using effective fire and movement tactics and deploying a smoke screen, Major Gordon Brown's D Company managed to reach the walls of the abbey, where it was joined by elements of A Company. This prompted a withdrawal by the surviving SS defenders, who covered their retreat with a powerful artillery bombardment. The following morning, the Regina Rifles moved forward again, consolidating the vacated and badly damaged buildings and the orchards beyond. Albeit at great cost, 3rd Division's tasks in the opening phases of Operation Charnwood had been fulfilled.

ENDING THE TOUR: To return to Caen, rejoin the D220c and follow it south-east into the city centre.

TOUR C

11TH ARMOURED DIVISION, BRAS & HUBERT-FOLIE

OBJECTIVE: This tour covers 11th Armoured Division's attack on the first day of Operation 'Goodwood', focusing on the leading unit, 3rd Royal Tank Regiment (3rd RTR). It also examines the capture of the villages of Bras and Hubert-Folie on 19 July.

DURATION/SUITABILITY: The tour lasts half a day, with a total distance of 22 km. The terrain is undemanding and the roads (apart from the N13) fairly quiet; the tour is therefore suitable for cyclists. Tourers with mobility difficulties may wish to avoid Stand C1, and begin at Stand C2 instead.

Stand C1: Escoville

DIRECTIONS: The village of Escoville lies 4 km east of the Orne, about 9 km from central Caen. It is probably best to use a road atlas to reach the general area, and then refer to the tour map. To complicate matters, there have recently been several changes to the road system which do not appear on any maps. With a little patience, however, Escoville is relatively easy to find. Once there,

0
1
Kilometres
Longueval
St-Léonard
Poste Électrique de Ranville
Val Marais
le Four à Chaux
Val St-Laurent
le Château
Escoville
Ferme de Beauvoisin
Ste-Honorine la Chardonnette
l'Ormelet
le Moulin à Vent
St-Pierre-St-Paul
COLOMBELLES
le Pré Baron
les Crêtes St-Samson
Rond-Point Lazzaro
Delle des Terres Noires
Delle des Rougelles
Butte de la Hogue
le Noir Val
D226
Parc d'Activités Lazzaro
la Fosse Guillaume
le Clos du Houx
Cuverville
Beaumont
le Clos à la Dame
Touffréville
la Grue
les Carrières
la Malicorne
la Vallée d'Enfer
D226
le Mont
le Clos des Prés
la Mare
le Petit Vallon
Démouville
Giberville
le Marais Grondin
le Bout de Là-Bas
les Carrières
la Fontaine
Lirose
le Malassis
le Platane
le Grand Pendant
To CAEN
N175
le Clos Neuf
le Clos de la Tête
le Martray
Commune de Banneville-la-
Aire de Service de Giberville Nord
Autoroute de
A13
Aire de Service de Giberville Sud
la Haie de Saules
Manneville Haras
le Prieuré Ferme
le Mesnil Frémentel
le Bas Mesnil
N13
D228
la Colombe
To CAGNY
l'Etoile
C1
C2
C3
C4
C5
C6
C7
① 29th Armoured Brigade, 0745 - 0915 hours 18 July
② 3rd RTR, 0915 - 0930 hours 18 July
③ 2nd Fife and Forfar Yeomanry
④ 3rd Monmouths, 0745 - 1000 hours 18 July
⑤ 1st Herefords, 0830 - 1000 hours 18 July
⑥ 3rd Monmouths, 1210 - 1500 hours 18 July
⑦ British minefield, showing gaps cleared by Royal Engineers
Base map: IGN 1612OT

park near the church and walk along the road towards Ste-Honorine la Chardronette. After 200 metres turn onto a farm track beside the hedgerow to your right. Continue for 600 metres until you reach a grassy path heading uphill on your left. Stop here.

THE SITE: In July 1944 the track along which you have just walked ran through a minefield laid by 51st (Highland) Division, which helped defend the Orne Bridgehead after D-Day. Owing to problems in locating the mines, only about 20 gaps were cleared through this obstacle before Goodwood began. Two of these 13-metre-wide gaps were at the south-west corner of Escoville, with another in the middle of the track along which you have just walked, and a fourth where you are now standing. On 18 July the entire strength of 29th Armoured Brigade, 5th Guards Armoured Brigade and 22nd Armoured Brigade had to pass through these gaps before attacking south. This meant that VIII Corps' armour entered the fighting piecemeal, weakening its offensive impact and limiting the number of objectives that could be attacked simultaneously.

Looking west, the fields from here to St-Honorine provided the jumping-off point for 159th Infantry Brigade, 11th Armoured Division's other main fighting component. From this stand you can see the restricted frontage from which VIII Corps began Operation Goodwood, and imagine the congestion experienced by the attackers as they passed through their own minefield.

THE ACTION: After concentrating east of the River Orne on 16–17 July, at around 0100 hours on the 18th the personnel of 11th Armoured Division were told that Operation Goodwood was 'on'. A few hours later, the armoured regiments began moving to their start line. Lt-Col David Silvertop's 3rd RTR led, accompanied by G Company, 8th Rifle Brigade (G/8th) in its armoured half-tracks, eight Sexton self-propelled 25-pounder guns from H Battery, 13th Royal Horse Artillery (H/13th RHA), and various vehicles from attached units. 2nd Fife and Forfar Yeomanry's regimental group (including F/8th Rifle Brigade and I/13th RHA) followed, with 23rd Hussars (plus H/8th Rifle Brigade and G/13th RHA) bringing up the rear.

Soon after the bombing began at 0545 hours, 3rd RTR moved through the minefield into the fields beyond. A Squadron, commanded by Major Bill Close, was on the right (west), with

Major John Watts' B Squadron on the left. Each squadron deployed in box formation, with two troops of four Shermans apiece forward and two behind, plus squadron headquarters (three tanks) in the middle. Behind these 38 tanks came the four Shermans of regimental headquarters, together with the regimental reconnaissance troop, G/8th Rifle Brigade's carrier platoon and some mine-clearing flail tanks from A Squadron, 22nd Dragoon Guards. Three AVREs from 26th Assault Squadron, RE, each mounting a 290-mm petard mortar, were also with this group. Last came 3rd RTR's C Squadron (19 Shermans), H/13th RHA and the rest of G/8th Rifle Brigade. The whole regimental group comprised around 150 vehicles, most of them tracked or semi-tracked.

Escoville. The eastern end of the track to Stand C1, with Ste-Honorine la Chardronette on the left. *(SCT)*

According to 3rd RTR's war diary, the regiment reached its forming-up positions south of the minefield by 0700 hours. Unfortunately, this placed it partly within the area to be covered by the rolling artillery barrage that was to begin shortly afterwards. When the guns opened up at 0745 hours, a number of rounds fell short. Some tanks reversed towards the start line, disrupting their formation. More seriously, several tank commanders were out of their vehicles when the first shells landed. Major Peter Burr, commanding C Squadron, was killed, as were two lieutenants. This represented an inauspicious start to a day that was to get much worse for the men of 11th Armoured Division's leading regiment.

Stand C2: The track to Cuverville

DIRECTIONS: Walk south along the grassy track to the Escoville–Ste-Honorine road, which runs along the crest of a low ridge. Cross the road and continue 100 metres south.

THE SITE: You are now standing in the no-man's-land between the line held by British troops before Operation Goodwood, and the northern edge of the German outpost zone. On a clear day you can pick out villages on the Bourguébus Ridge about 9 km further away. A maelstrom of smoke and fire covered this entire area on the morning of 18 July, as over 1,900 British and American aircraft, assisted by hundreds of artillery pieces, deluged thousands of tons of high explosive onto the German positions in front of you.

Look along the track to Cuverville, which was heavily bombed and shelled early on 18 July. It was then attacked by 3rd Battalion, The Monmouthshire Regiment, assisted by Cromwell tanks from A Squadron, 2nd Northamptonshire Yeomanry (11th Armoured Division's recce regiment). Most of the post-war expansion of Cuverville has been on its southern side, and the surrounding fields have changed little since 1944. Consequently, you can still get an excellent idea of the distance covered by 3rd Monmouths. Looking south-east from Stand C2, 3rd RTR's forming up area was a few hundred metres away. It was from here that the regiment set off towards its objective at Beauvoir Farm, 11 km to the south-west.

THE ACTION: Despite the disruption caused by its own supporting artillery, 3rd RTR advanced soon after H-Hour, following the barrage south. 29th Armoured Brigade's Tactical Headquarters and 2nd Fife and Forfar Yeomanry followed, creating room for 23rd Hussars to pass through the minefield. Last through the gaps was 8th Rifle Brigade's HQ group, accompanied by a troop of engineers from 612th Field Squadron, RE, and twelve M10 tank destroyers from 75th Anti-Tank Regiment, RA.

German resistance in the opening stages of the assault was negligible. Those members of 16th *Luftwaffe* Field Division unlucky enough to have been caught in the open during the bombardment were dead or incapacitated, and 8th Rifle Brigade's motor companies rounded up many prisoners. There was little opposition

from either flank. On 29th Armoured Brigade's right, the garrison of Cuverville was already under attack from 3rd Monmouths. Further east, Touffréville's defenders were in better condition, having mostly been missed by the bombing. However, the village was in a hollow, which meant that the Germans were unable easily to bring their weapons to bear against the British tanks.

> **Those problems that were encountered resulted mainly from inaccurate Allied bombing:**
>
> 'There was no hope of keeping a tidy formation. Our orders were to stick as close to [the barrage] as possible and for the first few hundred yards we seemed to be catching up nicely. Then we ran into fields of craters hidden in a brownish fog which hung over everything. They were shallow, but some of them must have been 40 feet across with the edges of the consistency of cocoa [powder]. They would have been no bother if we could have seen them coming but they were filled with fumes and almost invisible. Any tank that went in at the wrong angle was likely to capsize. All around me I could hear engines whining as drivers changed down to crawl over the obstacles. The barrage thundered away, spouting smoking clouds above this awful sea of powdery soil.'
>
> *Source:* William Moore, *Panzer Bait – With the 3rd Royal Tank Regiment 1940–1944*, p. 142.

Stand C3: Cuverville

DIRECTIONS: Walk back along the road to Escoville, rejoin your vehicle and drive into the village. Then turn right onto the D227, signposted Touffréville and Sannerville. At the crossroads 300 metres south of Escoville turn right onto the D228 to Cuverville. You are now driving through the area occupied by I/46th *Luftwaffe* Rifles on 18 July. At the T-junction in Cuverville turn left onto the D226 and then right, back onto the D228. After 300 metres park beside Cuverville's battle-scarred church, which in 1944 marked the southern edge of the village.

THE ACTION: While the armour moved down the 'corridor' west of Touffréville, Brigadier Jack Churcher's 159th Brigade launched its attack against Cuverville and Démouville. The assault was led by 3rd Monmouths' A and B Companies.

Although they came under sporadic artillery and machine-gun fire, Cuverville was entered by 0835 hours and secured by around 1000 hours. Some 50 prisoners were taken, mostly from 16th *Luftwaffe* Field Division.

Cuverville seen from Stand C2, with the woods near la Hogue on the horizon. *(SCT)*

Stand C4: Démouville

DIRECTIONS: Leave Cuverville and continue towards Démouville. II/46th *Luftwaffe* Rifles' command post was located just north of the current boundary of Démouville, on the right-hand (west) side of the road; the battalion commander and his staff were captured near here. About 500 metres east of the D228 there is an area of hedges and trees, which was cleared by 1st Battalion, The Herefordshire Regiment, (also from 159th Infantry Brigade) and C Squadron, 2nd Northants Yeomanry, in an attack beginning at 0830 hours. About 70 prisoners were taken here, again mostly from 16th *Luftwaffe* Field Division.

Drive into Démouville and park near the church.

THE SITE: In 1944 Démouville was surrounded by orchards. The village was more strongly defended than Cuverville, notably by about 10 self-propelled anti-tank guns and howitzers from 1/200th Assault Gun Battalion (21st Panzer Division). However,

Then: Soldiers of 1st/7th Queen's Regiment (7th Armoured Division) comb through the ruined village of Démouville on 19 July. *(IWM B7754)*

Now: A modern view of Démouville church, seen from the west. *(SCT)*

the bombing destroyed most of these weapons before British troops arrived. According to several accounts, the church tower was used by German snipers during the battle for the village.

THE ACTION: After clearing Cuverville, 3rd Monmouths was supposed to hand it over to a battalion of the Highland Division before attacking Démouville. However, a German artillery concentration caused the handover to be postponed, and the assault only began at 1210 hours. This time the Monmouths' C and D Companies led, supported by an artillery barrage and by C Squadron, 2nd Northants Yeomanry. The Yeomanry knocked out two self-propelled guns in an orchard at Démouville's northern edge, and the infantry entered the village. Although some Germans escaped to Giberville (where most were later rounded up by Canadian troops), by 1435 hours 159th Brigade was reporting Démouville clear apart from three small pockets. Assisted by a company from 5th Coldstream Guards, by 1500 hours these were mopped up, and 3rd Monmouths dug in. 159th Brigade's third battalion, 4th King's Shropshire Light Infantry (4th KSLI), advanced in support to a position east of Démouville. Later, Brigadier Churcher ordered another move forward, and by 2000 hours all three battalions were digging in around le Mesnil Frémentel, 2 km further south.

159th Infantry Brigade's performance on 18 July was creditable. However, its advance demonstrated considerable caution on the part of Brigadier Churcher. In fairness, his decisions reflected Montgomery's directive of 15 July, which stressed the importance of maintaining a secure east flank for the Normandy bridgehead, and – by implication – of consolidating objectives as they were captured. Still, the fact remains that at a time when 29th and 5th Guards Armoured Brigades desperately needed infantry to capture villages on both sides of the Caen–Vimont railway, VIII Corps' leading infantry brigade was unavailable. The consequences of this deficiency are addressed at other stands in this tour, and in Tour D.

Stand C5: The old railway line

DIRECTIONS: Continue along the D228 to the roundabout on the N175. Turn left and drive 1.5 km before turning left into a parking area beside the road (note the 'no entry' sign at the exit, 200 metres before the entrance). Stop and walk 100 metres east alongside the N175. Here you will find one of the best-preserved sections of the single-track railway that ran from Caen to Troarn in 1944 (the track itself has been removed, but the embankment sides remain).

Stand C5, looking east with the N175 on the right and the path of the old railway line in the centre. *(SCT)*

THE ACTION: Soon after 0800 hours, 3rd RTR's leading elements reached the Caen–Troarn railway (codenamed 'Matilda'). Here, 29th Armoured Brigade was to turn south-west, heading towards the Bourguébus Ridge west of Four. There was also supposed to be a pause in the rolling barrage at this point, to facilitate a crossing of the railway and the deployment of 2nd Fife and Forfar Yeomanry on 3rd RTR's left.

Most of the British tanks crossed the embankment successfully. However, the half-tracked and wheeled vehicles had problems. 26th Assault Squadron's AVREs were therefore called forward to blast gaps, and 612th Squadron RE improved the crossings. Meanwhile, at 0845 hours the second phase of the rolling barrage began, and 3rd RTR set off behind it, led once again by A Squadron.

Stand C6: le Mesnil Frémentel

DIRECTIONS: Retrace your route along the N175 to the roundabout south of Démouville and turn left onto the D228. Park beyond the bridge across the A13, and walk back for views over

the battlefield. Then continue towards Cagny. About 750 metres before the village turn right at a crossroads towards the hamlet of le Mesnil Frémentel. Pull over after 25 metres and look front right to a wall and hedgerow running north. This marks the eastern boundary of a large field through which 3rd RTR advanced south.

THE SITE: On 18 July le Mesnil Frémentel was the HQ of I/125th Panzergrenadier Regiment, whose command post was in the farmyard north of the road running through the hamlet. Le Mesnil was defended mainly by 3/125th Panzergrenadiers and the heavy weapons of 4th Company. Nearby was 4/200th Assault Gun Battalion. Its four 75-mm self-propelled anti-tank guns were deployed astride the D228, with the battery's six 105-mm howitzers 500 metres behind them in the orchards at Cagny.

Le Mesnil Frémentel, looking south from the D228. Aerial photographs taken on 18 July show that 3rd RTR moved through (indeed, probably created) the large gap in the hedge seen in the middle of the photo. *(SCT)*

THE ACTION: Le Mesnil Frémentel was heavily bombed and shelled early on 18 July. According to 3/125th Panzergrenadiers' commander, many of the heavy weapons in the hamlet were destroyed, and the defenders' fighting spirit was severely shaken. Nevertheless, when 3rd RTR passed the hamlet a few hundred metres to the west at 0915 hours, several vehicles were knocked out by anti-tank guns emplaced here.

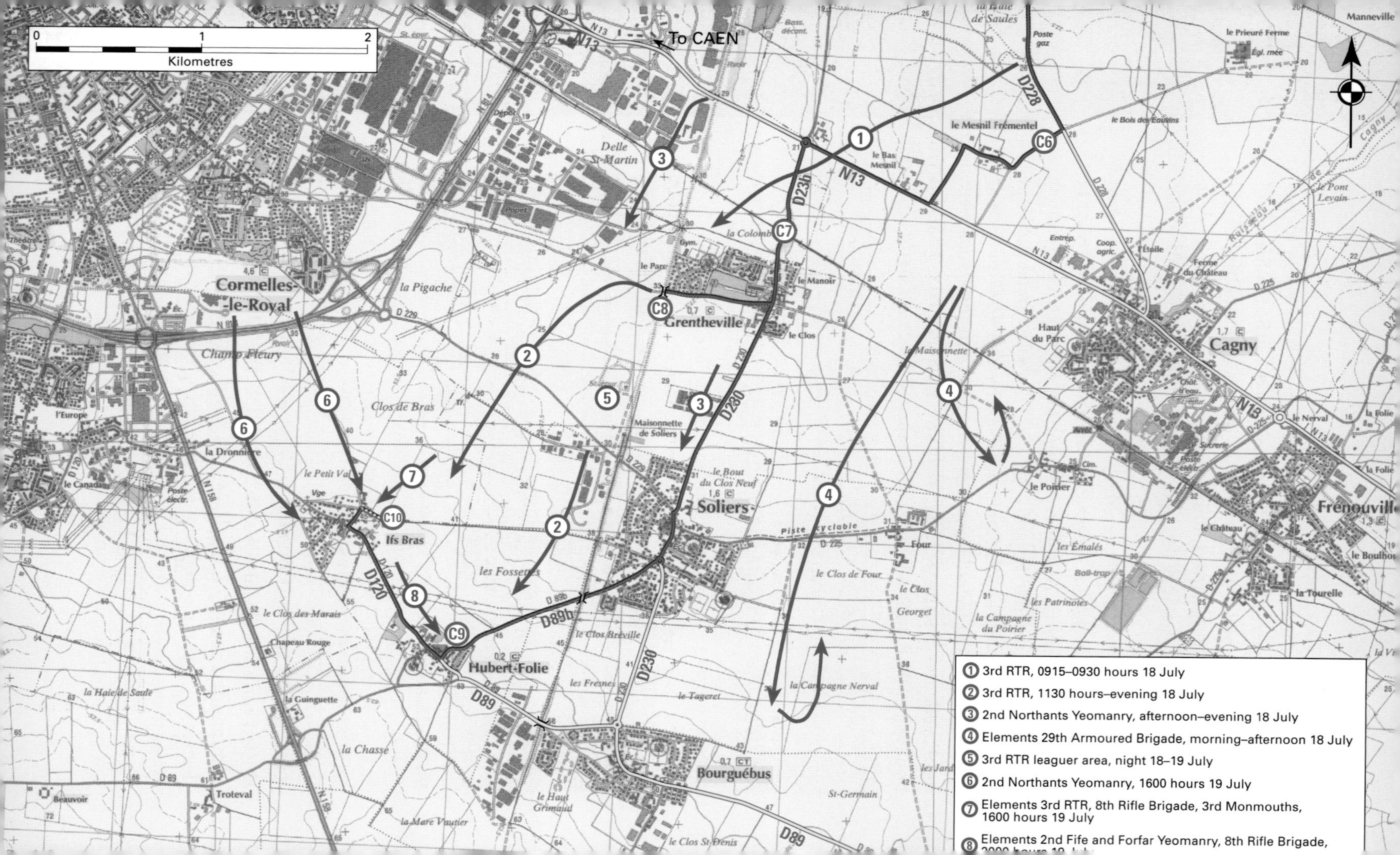
0
1
2
Kilometres
To CAEN
N13
D228
D23b
D230
D89b
D120
D89
C6
C7
C8
C9
C10
Cormelles-le-Royal
Grentheville
Cagny
Soliers
Frénouville
Hubert-Folie
Bourguébus
Ifs Bras
le Mesnil Frémentel
Delle St-Martin
la Pigache
Clos de Bras
Champ Fleury
la Dronnière
le Petit Val
les Fossettes
Maisonnette de Soliers
le Bout du Clos Neuf
le Poirier
le Clos de Four
la Campagne Nerval
la Campagne du Poirier
les Patrinotes
les Émalés
le Château
la Tourelle
le Nerval
Haut du Parc
la Colombe
le Manoir
le Clos
le Bas Mesnil
le Bois des Eauvins
le Prieuré Ferme
Manneville
la Chasse
la Guinguette
Chapeau Rouge
le Clos des Marais
la Haie de Saule
la Mare Vautier
Troteval
Beauvoir
le Haut Grimaud
le Clos St-Denis
St-Germain
les Fresnes
le Tageret
le Clos Bréville
le Clos Georget
Piste cyclable
① 3rd RTR, 0915–0930 hours 18 July
② 3rd RTR, 1130 hours–evening 18 July
③ 2nd Northants Yeomanry, afternoon–evening 18 July
④ Elements 29th Armoured Brigade, morning–afternoon 18 July
⑤ 3rd RTR leaguer area, night 18–19 July
⑥ 2nd Northants Yeomanry, 1600 hours 19 July
⑦ Elements 3rd RTR, 8th Rifle Brigade, 3rd Monmouths, 1600 hours 19 July
⑧ Elements 2nd Fife and Forfar Yeomanry, 8th Rifle Brigade,

Having lost one of his Shermans, Major Close wanted to stop and deal with the enemy. However, 3rd RTR's squadrons were under orders to press on to their objective. They therefore continued towards Grentheville, leaving le Mesnil Frémentel behind them.

Hearing of the problems encountered at le Mesnil, Brigadier C.B.C. ('Roscoe') Harvey, commanding 29th Armoured Brigade, instructed 23rd Hussars to capture the hamlet. However, the Hussars were caught up in fighting near le Prieuré farm and were unable to assist. The task therefore fell to 8th Rifle Brigade's HQ group, commanded by the 28-year-old Lt-Col Tony Hunter. Assisted by the M10s of 75th Anti-Tank Regiment's 119th Battery, plus around a dozen flail tanks and AVREs, at 1030 hours the attack began. It was led by two of 8th Rifle Brigade's machine-gun platoons, which dismounted from their carriers on the edge of the hamlet. They encountered little resistance, and spent several hours rounding up prisoners. Over 130 Germans were captured here, mainly from I/125th Panzergrenadiers.

Stand C7: Grentheville railway bridge

DIRECTIONS: Follow the road through le Mesnil Frémentel to the N13. Turn right and after 800 metres turn left at a roundabout onto the D230. Cross the Caen–Vimont railway and immediately pull into a parking area on the left. Walk back to the bridge (be careful; there is no pavement) and look north-west and north-east.

THE ACTION: After crossing the N13, 3rd RTR reached the fields near Grentheville at 0930 hours. This area was occupied by about 20 *Nebelwerfer* multiple rocket launchers and several anti-tank guns. The most serious opposition, however, came from the self-propelled pieces of 3/200th Assault Gun Battalion, deployed in the orchards and woods surrounding Grentheville.

3rd RTR's arrival caused panic among the *Nebelwerfer* crews, several of whose projectors were crushed under the tracks of the Shermans. G/8th Rifle Brigade also helped mop up opposition in this area, taking numerous prisoners before pushing on.

***Leutnant* Wild, commanding 1st Troop, 14th Werfer Regiment at Grentheville, described his experience:**

'[Wild] stated that during the period he was at the front he fired only once, just before his Troop was overrun by Allied tanks... When he felt his position was about to be overrun he requested permission from [1st] Battalion to withdraw. This was refused. When he tried to get in touch with Battalion a second time he could make no contact. When Allied tanks... were 300 metres in front of his position he told his men to clear out and remained in his Troop position until overrun.'

Source: Combined Services Detailed Interrogation Centre report SIR 631, 30 July 1944, UK National Archives.

Stand C8: Grentheville railway embankment

DIRECTIONS: Rejoin your vehicle and continue south past the liberation memorial on your right (Grentheville was captured by F and H Companies, 8th Rifle Brigade, later on 18 July). At the next roundabout turn right and drive 600 metres towards the railway embankment, which in 1944 carried an industrial line to Colombelles. Turn right and park before the underpass. Then walk up the path onto the embankment. From here, look south towards the villages of Hubert-Folie and Ifs Bras (known simply as Bras in 1944), visible on the horizon 2.5 km away.

The liberation monument beside the D230 in Grentheville. *(SCT)*

THE ACTION: Despite its success in overrunning the *Nebelwerfer* positions, 3rd RTR came under intense fire as it approached Grentheville. A Squadron claimed to have hit several self-propelled guns, but at least five of its own tanks were knocked out; B and C Squadrons also suffered losses. In response, H/13th RHA put down a covering bombardment, and the British tanks moved closer to the railway embankment.

Lt-Col Silvertop was determined to avoid becoming bogged down at Grentheville, and ordered A Squadron to cross the embankment. Major Close responded by moving his tank towards the underpass near where you are standing.

Major Close described what happened next:

'The embankment was high and steep, and I didn't want to scramble over the top, where we would be silhouetted. But there were a few openings... under the railway, so I told my chaps to get through the nearest one and into cover on the far side. But despite several attempts to get them to move, nothing happened... I stood up in my tank, took off my beret, waved it above my head, ordered 'Conform to me' on the radio and shot up the nearest hole like a rat up a drainpipe. As I did so I remember hoping it wasn't mined. There was no time to worry about that, and fortunately it wasn't. To a man the squadron followed and we emerged onto the far side, into a scene of absolute peace and calm. No sign of enemy or war, just an ocean of golden corn, waving gently in the breeze... I remember thinking "This is it. This is where we really get going." But how wrong I was.'

Source: Christopher Dunphie, *The Pendulum of Battle*, p. 88.

The underpass at Stand C8 is one of several providing passage between the two sides of the old industrial railway leading south from Colombelles. *(SCT)*

Followed by other vehicles of the regiment, A Squadron continued towards the factory area of Cormelles, before halting while a patrol was sent to reconnoitre Hubert-Folie. This unenviable task fell to Lieutenant David Stileman, commanding a platoon of G/8th Rifle Brigade. Taking two carriers, he motored along the west side of the embankment, hidden by crops, to a position near Soliers. Then, following a flurry of shells from H/13th RHA, he dashed along the road through Hubert-Folie before emerging to the west and heading back down the slope. Having received Stileman's report that the village appeared unoccupied, Silvertop ordered his tanks to advance. Their objective, a spot height (Point 72) at Beauvoir Farm, was only 4 km away. The time was approximately 1100 hours.

View looking south-west from Stand C8, with Bras right and Hubert-Folie left on the horizon. Apart from a few buildings near the embankment, this area is almost unchanged since July 1944. *(SCT)*

Stand C9: Hubert-Folie

DIRECTIONS: Drive back to the roundabout in Grentheville. Turn right and continue into Soliers. Turn left at the T-junction and immediately bear right by the church. At the next roundabout take the first exit, the D89b, and follow the road through the underpass to Hubert-Folie. Park by the church, walk back to the north-eastern edge of the village, and look across the fields to the north.

THE SITE: Unlike Démouville and Cuverville, Hubert-Folie has changed relatively little since the war. There is a monument to the village's liberation at its most south-easterly point, beside the road to Bourguébus.

Although the evidence is incomplete, Lieutenant Stileman's report that Hubert-Folie was unoccupied on the morning of 18 July appears to have been incorrect. Nevertheless, whether or not the village was strongly held, the Bourguébus Ridge as a whole was well defended, and the Germans could bring many weapons to bear west of the railway embankment. As well as 21st Panzer Division's engineer and anti-tank battalions, a small number of 88-mm anti-aircraft guns was available. Some of these were organised into *Flakkampftruppen*, which were specifically intended for ground combat. Some self-propelled guns from 155th Panzer Artillery Regiment were also west of the north–south railway line. By midday they were reinforced by 2/200th Assault Gun Battalion, which withdrew from Giberville. During the afternoon part of 1st SS Panzer Division's Panther battalion reached this area, where it was joined later by most of 1st SS Assault Gun Battalion. During the evening III/1st SS Panzergrenadier Regiment took possession of Bras, and by the next day I/1st SS Panzergrenadiers had occupied Hubert-Folie. Together, these units represented a formidable obstacle to 11th Armoured Division's drive south.

THE ACTION: In accordance with Silvertop's instructions, at roughly 1130 hours on 18 July 3rd RTR began its final push towards Beauvoir Farm. A Squadron was on the right, with B Squadron nearer the railway line. However, about 500 metres from Hubert-Folie and Bras, the British came under heavy fire, apparently from all directions.

> **Major Close's tank was among the first to be hit:**
>
> 'I lost four tanks in a matter of moments. There was a hell of a crack and someone shouted "Bale out, sir", so I hopped down and saw that a shot had neatly removed the rear sprocket and the track was cut in two… I sent the crew back to the shelter of the embankment and ran over to my remaining squadron HQ tanks. One had been knocked out but the other was all right, so I sent the corporal [tank commander] back and took over command of the squadron again. On my left the rest of the battalion was heavily engaged, at least seven tanks blazing, and knocked-out crews dotting the landscape as they made their way back to the embankment.'
>
> *Source:* William Moore, *Panzer Bait – With the 3rd Royal Tank Regiment 1940–1944*, p. 147.

Completely exposed on the open slopes north of Hubert-Folie, 3rd RTR was unable to respond effectively to the German fire. Several tanks pushed briefly across the D120 east of Bras (*see photo p. 81*), but attempts to continue the advance only led to further losses. Furthermore, by early afternoon it was obvious that the German units were being reinforced.

> **Sergeant 'Buck' Kite described 1st SS Panzer Regiment's arrival:**
>
> 'Suddenly, from a small copse on top of the ridge to my right there were gun flashes, and I could see a tank taking up a firing position. I engaged what I think was a Panther, and I saw the crew bale out… There seemed to be more tanks appearing on the ridge, and I knocked out another. But it was now getting very sticky, and we were ordered to pull back slowly, which we did, making best use of the ground – not easy in that open country.'
>
> *Source:* Christopher Dunphie, *The Pendulum of Battle*, pp. 95–6.

For several hours individual tanks and troops jockeyed for position, hoping to find a weak spot in the defences. But despite instructions to keep advancing, at 1545 hours 3rd RTR's remaining Shermans started falling back. During the late afternoon elements of 2nd Northants Yeomanry – now freed from their infantry support role – came up, with instructions to renew the assault. However, they too suffered losses, and reported at 1945 hours that they were in defensive positions west of the embankment. Thanks to effective artillery support and frequent interventions by Typhoon fighter-bombers, all attempts by the Germans to counter-attack down the slope were broken up. However, by mid-evening it was clear that VIII Corps' offensive had been halted, and 3rd RTR was ordered to consolidate. Although shots were exchanged until last light, at 2230 hours Silvertop's battered regiment leaguered 1.5 km north-east of Hubert-Folie, still to the west of the railway embankment. By then, of 61 tanks with which 3rd RTR had started the day, only 4 Fireflies and 16 'standard' 75-mm Shermans were fit to fight. Fortunately, personnel casualties were rather less heavy. Even so, according to 29th Armoured Brigade's war diary, 48 officers and men had been killed or wounded. By any reasonable standards, these were still grievous losses.

Soliers and the north–south railway embankment, midday 18 July. Numerous vehicles of the 3rd RTR regimental group can be seen west of the embankment. An interesting feature of this photograph is that it shows that (contrary to most reports) some vehicles went over the top of the embankment (see top left), rather than through the road underpasses, two of which can be seen near Soliers.
(Keele University Air Photo Archive)

Stand C10: Ifs Bras

DIRECTIONS: Turn right at Hubert-Folie church onto the D89. 100 metres further on, turn right again (effectively, straight ahead) onto the D120. Continue into the next village, which a signpost identifies as Ifs, but is actually Bras. Turn right at the stop sign and park near the crossroads. Walk down the Chemin de Soliers, which brings you to the northern edge of the village.

THE ACTION: Following the disappointments of 18 July, on the next day VIII Corps restricted itself to set-piece battles to capture a number of settlements along the Bourguébus Ridge. After consultation between Dempsey, O'Connor and the divisional commanders, it was decided that the attacks would begin at 1600 hours, when 11th Armoured Division would assault Bras. Since 2nd Northants Yeomanry was reasonably intact, it was agreed that its Cromwells should spearhead the attack, assisted by two companies from 8th Rifle Brigade and supported by a powerful artillery bombardment. 159th Infantry Brigade would also be brought forward, to defend the villages when they were taken.

Early on 19 July C Squadron, 2nd Northants Yeomanry, and some Inns of Court Regiment armoured cars reconnoitred towards Cormelles, prompting the withdrawal of a few German vehicles from the woods south of the village. The rest of the Northants Yeomanry then moved to Cormelles, where they assembled for their attack. German troops were seen digging in north of Bras and Hubert-Folie, and were shelled in preparation for the assault. Meanwhile, 3rd RTR withdrew to a position north of Grentheville, where it received some replacement Shermans, and the regiment was reorganised into two squadrons, each with about a dozen tanks. 3rd RTR then returned to the west side of the embankment, where it had been allocated the role (with G/8th Rifle Brigade) of capturing Hubert-Folie once Bras had fallen.

At 1600 hours the attack began, with 2nd Northants Yeomanry advancing behind a smoke screen, C Squadron on the right, A on the left and B in reserve. Some of the tanks strayed towards the German positions around Ifs and were knocked out. Fearing a loss of momentum, Lt-Col Silvertop suggested that his own regiment should take over the attack. Brigadier Harvey agreed, and 3rd RTR advanced, closely followed by F/ and H/8th Rifle Brigade in their

half-tracks. Almost simultaneously, the leading troops of 3rd Monmouths (A and D Companies) appeared through the corn to the north, having suffered casualties to German artillery fire, but still determined to fight. Despite its losses, 2nd Northants Yeomanry also continued to close in on Bras from the west.

Disrupted by the preliminary bombardment, and struck from several directions by tanks and infantry, the German defences broke. Although it took some time to clear the village, by 1800 hours Bras was firmly in British hands. The defenders lost 200–300 men, mainly from III/1st SS Panzergrenadier Regiment. 11th Armoured Division's losses were considerably lower, although some tanks were knocked out and 3rd RTR was once again reduced to skeleton strength.

The view north from Stand C10, showing the exposed area across which British forces attacked on 18–19 July. *(SCT)*

Obersturmführer (Lieutenant) Zelinka, an officer in 9/1st SS Panzergrenadiers, described the collapse:

'There was heavy preparatory fire, then the enemy broke through... The point of breakthrough lay in the sector held by the unit adjacent to us to the left. From this position the enemy attempted to attack our battalion in the flank and

rear. Hidden from the enemy by the tall grain, most of the company to our left managed to pull back to the positions held by the reserve company. Most of our company, however, lay on completely exposed terrain. With a huge number of enemy tanks moving towards us, most of the company stayed put. Additional enemy tanks arrived and succeeded in penetrating the village of Bras from both flanks. The enemy infantry soon followed. With that, it became impossible for us to pull back... Only a few individuals made it back to the battalion. Those were the men who were in the village of Bras itself or who had managed to hide somewhere until dark.'

Source: Rudolf Lehmann & Ralf Tiemann, *The Leibstandarte*, Vol. 4 Part 1, pp. 159–60.

At about 2000 hours, the British followed up their success with an attack on Hubert-Folie. This took time to organise, not least because of the need to bring up 2nd Fife and Forfar Yeomanry to replace 3rd RTR, which was incapable of further offensive action. However, after a ten-minute artillery bombardment the British moved forward, hidden by a smoke screen fired by 8th Rifle Brigade's mortars and assisted by a flanking move to the west by 2nd Northants Yeomanry. Resistance in Hubert-Folie, which seems to have been mostly evacuated by I/1st SS Panzergrenadiers before the assault, was sporadic, and the village was soon cleared; G/8th Rifle Brigade took about 50 prisoners. 4th KSLI then moved forward to relieve the assault force, suffering casualties to several surviving machine gunners around Hubert-Folie in the process. By midnight, however, with 159th Brigade (plus supporting anti-tank and other weapons) dug in around Bras and Hubert-Folie, the situation was regarded as stable enough to allow 29th Armoured Brigade to be withdrawn. After a costly and difficult two days, its participation in Operation Goodwood was over.

The view north-east from Stand D1, with Soliers (*left*), Cagny and le Poirier (*right*) and Four obscured by trees in the centre. 2nd Fife and Forfar Yeomanry suffered heavy losses in these fields as its tanks tried to climb towards Bourguébus. *(SCT)*

TO CONCLUDE THE TOUR: Continue along the D120 from Bras for 750 metres and turn right onto the N158, which leads into Caen.

TO CONTINUE WITH TOUR D: Return to Hubert-Folie and exit the village on the D89 to the east, following the directions to Stand D1 given on p. 165.

TOUR D

THE SOUTH-EASTERN FLANK, 18–20 JULY

OBJECTIVE: This tour focuses on the south-eastern part of the Goodwood battlefield, where the Germans most feared a break-out. Owing to the complex nature of the fighting, the tour does not follow a chronological sequence, but instead offers a series of snapshots of the bitter struggle from 18–20 July.

DURATION/SUITABILITY: The tour lasts half a day, and can be combined with Tour C to make a full day. The total distance is

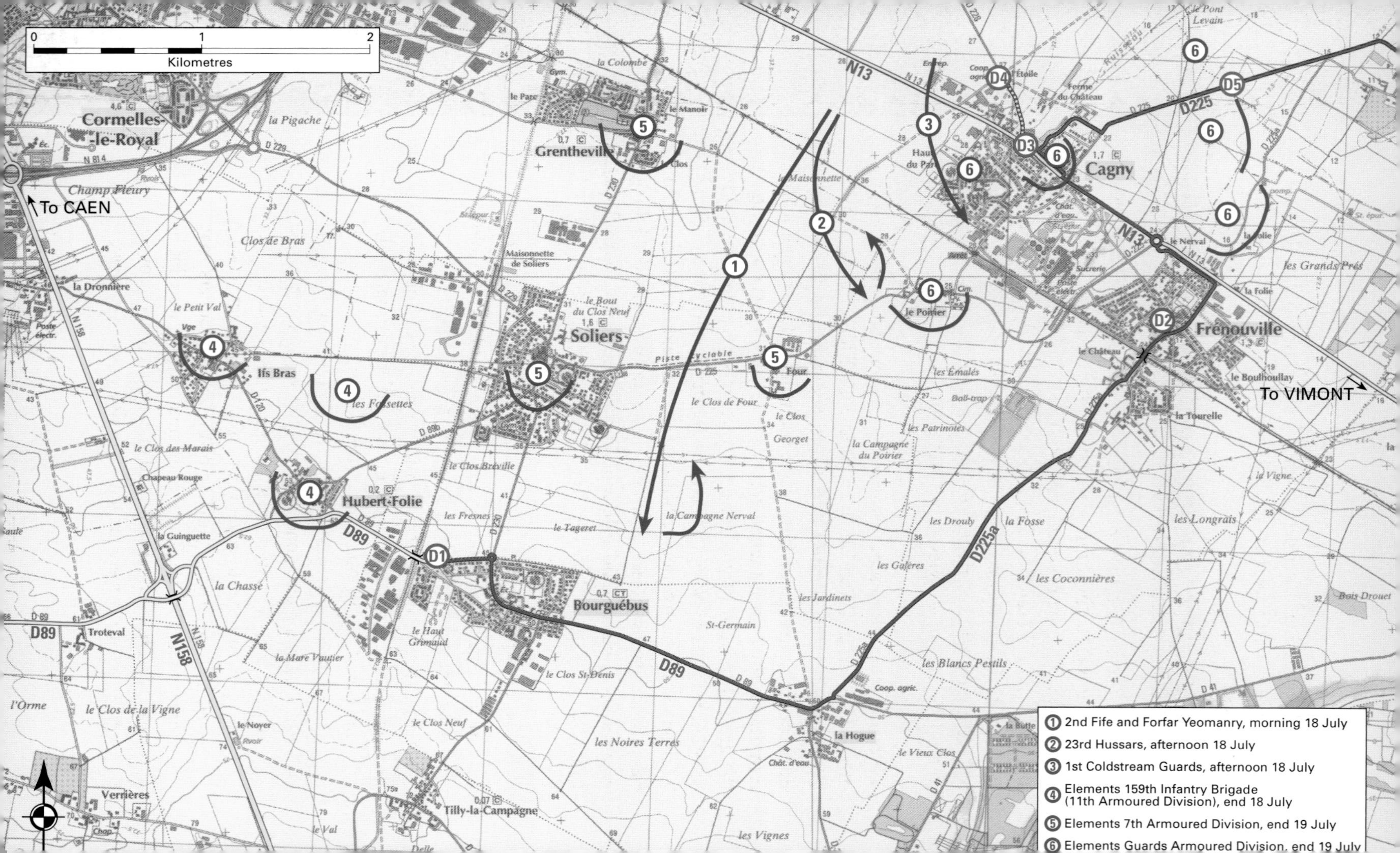

0 1 2 Kilometres
To CAEN
To VIMONT
Cormelles-le-Royal
Grentheville
Soliers
Ifs Bras
Hubert-Folie
Bourguébus
Cagny
Frénouville
Four
le Poirier
la Hogue
Tilly-la-Campagne
Verrières
Troteval
N13
N158
D89
D225
D225a
D1
D2
D3
D4
D5
① 2nd Fife and Forfar Yeomanry, morning 18 July
② 23rd Hussars, afternoon 18 July
③ 1st Coldstream Guards, afternoon 18 July
④ Elements 159th Infantry Brigade (11th Armoured Division), end 18 July
⑤ Elements 7th Armoured Division, end 19 July
⑥ Elements Guards Armoured Division, end 19 July

16 km. The terrain is gentle and the roads mostly quiet; the tour is therefore suitable for cyclists and those with mobility difficulties.

Stand D1: Bourguébus

DIRECTIONS: The tour begins at Bourguébus, the village that gave its name to the high ground at the heart of Operation Goodwood. To start the tour, leave Caen on the N158 to Falaise, and turn onto the D89 at la Guinguette. Pass Hubert-Folie and continue to the railway cutting 500 metres south-east of the village. Immediately after the bridge, turn right and park. Then walk back to the D89 for superb views over the battlefield.

THE SITE: From this position you can appreciate the strength of the German position on the Bourguébus Ridge. In particular, note how weapons located here could fire over the railway line into the fields north of Hubert-Folie, where elements of 11th Armoured Division attacked on 18–19 July. Observe also how the ground in front of you forms a concave slope, with few folds or other features to provide cover for an attacker.

Use the tour map to locate Soliers and the fields to the east. On 18 July the area between you and these features was the killing ground for most of 2nd Fife and Forfar Yeomanry, with 23rd Hussars being halted in the fields behind them, south of the Caen–Vimont railway.

Major Sir John Gilmour, commanding 2nd Fife and Forfar Yeomanry's B Squadron, described the moment when things went wrong:

'The day was fine and sunny and I could see our objective not far ahead... We shook out into tactical formation, passed Grentheville on our right, shooting up a number of *Nebelwerfers* in the woods there, and pressed on. Once my leading troops had gone about 6–700 yards south of the railway line, the rest of the squadron had to come out into the open, in order to cover them forward. Initially all went well, and we reached the line of the Four to Soliers road without real trouble. Then, quite suddenly, we were hit by heavy fire, first from Soliers and then from Four. Of course, while the enemy were in well concealed positions, we were completely exposed in open ground. Tanks all around started to brew and we found it almost impossible to get on.'

Source: Christopher Dunphie, *The Pendulum of Battle*, p. 99.

Stand D2: Frénouville

DIRECTIONS: Rejoin the D89 and drive east for 300 metres before turning right at a roundabout. Follow the road through Bourguébus and exit beyond the church. At 1115 hours on 18 July a troop of Fife and Forfar Shermans crossed the D89 some 300 metres east of the church, but was destroyed soon afterwards. If the road is quiet, pull over to examine the rising ground on your right. It was from this direction that 1st SS Panzer Division counter-attacked during the afternoon of 18 July. Rocket-firing Typhoons helped the surviving British armour to repel these attacks, but were unable to stop SS Panzergrenadiers from occupying Soliers, Four and le Poirier, from which the Germans were ejected in heavy fighting the next day.

Plaque commemorating the liberation of Frénouville, on the village church. *(SCT)*

Continue towards la Hogue, still held by II/2nd SS Panzergrenadiers at the end of the battle. Turn left before the 'Agrial' barn onto the D225a. After about 2 km enter Frénouville and bear left at the roundabout. Go through the railway underpass, past the château, and take the left fork before the church. Stop and note the plaque beside the church door, which celebrates the liberation of the village by 5th Battalion, The Coldstream Guards, on 20–21 July.

THE SITE: On 18 July 1944 Frénouville was the headquarters of Battlegroup *von Luck*, which took its name from *Major* Hans von Luck, its 33-year-old commander. In addition to von Luck's own 125th Panzergrenadier Regiment, the battlegroup comprised I/22nd Panzer Regiment, all five batteries of *Major* Alfred Becker's 200th Assault Gun Battalion and most of 21st Panzer Division's artillery. It also included attached elements of 16th *Luftwaffe* Field Division and 9th Werfer Brigade, plus 503rd

Heavy Panzer Battalion, with 39 operational Tiger or King Tiger tanks. With these forces *Major* von Luck was responsible for defending the central and eastern portions of the Goodwood battlefield, from Démouville and Touffréville in the north to the slopes of the Bourguébus Ridge in the south.

THE ACTION: After a weekend spent on leave in Paris, Hans von Luck left for his headquarters on Monday 17 July, intending to be back at his command post before dawn the next day. However, he was delayed by traffic jams and reached Frénouville only after the Allied air and artillery bombardment ended.

Hans von Luck, the highly experienced officer who did so much to organise the German defence against Operation Goodwood. The photo was taken after the battle, with von Luck wearing the Knight's Cross around his neck.

Major von Luck later recalled the scene at his HQ:

'The commander of I Battalion [125th Panzergrenadiers] greeted me briefly. I sensed that something was not right, for all the men at the command post seemed nervous. Then came the report that almost took my breath away.

"Since five o'clock this morning the British have been bombing our sector, especially the area of I Battalion, endlessly with thousands of bombers. This bombing was followed by a creeping barrage from the artillery. The firing stopped barely half an hour ago."

"How are things with your I Battalion, have you any news?" was my first question. "Not yet, we've no radio contact," came the answer.

"How about the Tigers and the panzer battalion of our regiment?" Answer: "No radio contact. I don't know how things look there."

"And II Battalion? Major Becker's assault guns? Have you told division?" My questions became more and more pressing, but it was clear that nothing had been done.

This was of course the renewed attempt at a breakout. Yet nothing, nothing at all, had been done! My deputy appeared to be in shock. He seemed absolutely helpless.'

Source: Hans von Luck, *Panzer Commander*, pp. 152–3.

Determined to discover what was happening, von Luck jumped into a Panzer IV command tank and ordered the driver to leave immediately in the direction of Caen. Their route took them through the village of Cagny, 1 km to the north-west.

Stand D3: Cagny church

DIRECTIONS: To follow von Luck's route, turn right just past Frénouville church and left at the crossroads. Continue 250 metres and bear sharp left onto a slip road, which brings you to a roundabout on the N13. Take the third exit towards Cagny and Caen. Continue into the centre of Cagny (which has grown considerably since 1944) and turn right onto a road running alongside the N13. Park and walk towards the church, stopping to read the information board near the post office, which contains an excellent map of Operation Goodwood. Then turn to face the open area behind the *mairie*, which seems the most likely location for the 88-mm flak battery mentioned below.

THE ACTION: Hans von Luck reached Cagny minutes after leaving his headquarters, and drove through the devastated village to its western edge. From here, he was shocked to see

Then: A Sherman recovery vehicle (*left*) prepares to tow a tank with a broken track outside the heavily-damaged Cagny church, 19 July. *(IWM B7796)*

Now: Cagny church today, looking west, with the area most probably occupied by the *Luftwaffe* flak battery in the field on the right. *(SCT)* dozens of British tanks and other vehicles crossing the N13 in front of him, while others approached from the north.

Realising that the defences to the north had been overrun, von Luck decided to return to Frénouville to organise counter-measures. Passing through Cagny, however, he noticed a battery of four 88-mm anti-aircraft guns (from III Flak Corps) near the church. He stopped his tank, ran across and ordered the *Luftwaffe* captain in charge to re-deploy his weapons to the edge of the village, from where they could hit the British armour from the flank. When the captain replied that his job was to fire at aircraft, von Luck drew his pistol and – according to his own account – gave the air force officer a choice between being shot and winning a medal. The captain decided to do as instructed, and accompanied von Luck to reconnoitre a position in an orchard at the northern edge of Cagny. Von Luck then promised to send reinforcements, and returned to his HQ, where he spent several hours co-ordinating his battlegroup's defence. Meanwhile, the *Luftwaffe* crews moved their cumbersome weapons to their new firing position.

Stand D4: Point 27, Cagny

DIRECTIONS: Walk to the church to see the commemorative plaques above the door. Then turn right onto the D228, the Route de Démouville. Walk past the buildings on both sides of the road; in 1944 most of this area was orchards. Stop at the road and farm track intersection on the north-western edge of Cagny.

THE SITE: You are now near the second location of the 88-mm battery. It is impossible to be certain of the guns' precise position, although many sources place them behind the stone wall of a nearby orchard, which you can still see several hundred metres to the east. It is interesting to consider the difference between the British response to the problems encountered at Cagny, as described below, and at le Mesnil Frémentel, discussed at Stand C6 (*pp. 150–3*) and visible only 750 metres away to the west.

THE ACTION: As described on p. 70, 11th Armoured Division's commander, Maj-Gen Roberts, had been given permission to by-pass Cagny during the early stages of his attack, and to leave its capture to the Guards Armoured Division. Consequently, at a time when the village was almost undefended,

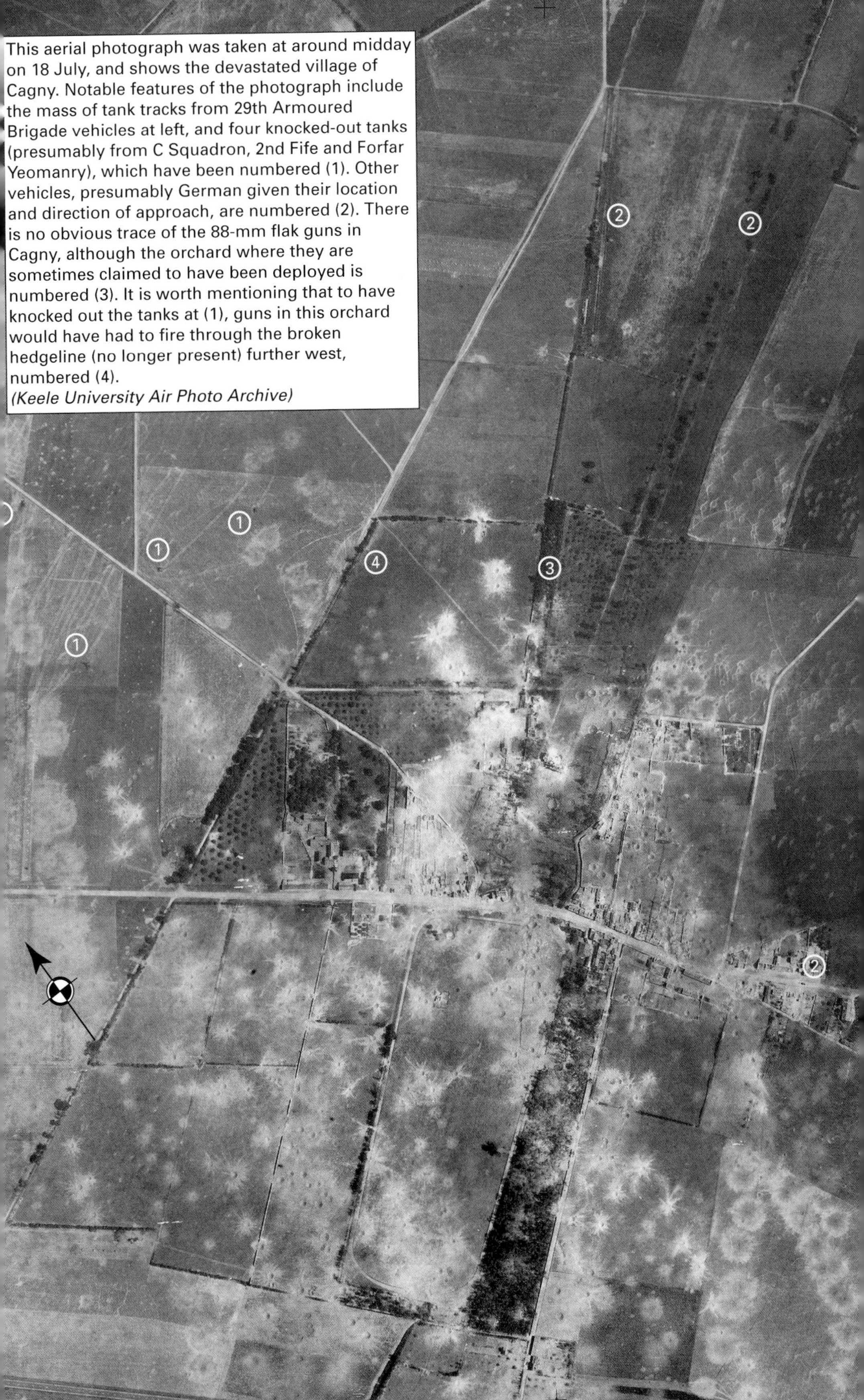

This aerial photograph was taken at around midday on 18 July, and shows the devastated village of Cagny. Notable features of the photograph include the mass of tank tracks from 29th Armoured Brigade vehicles at left, and four knocked-out tanks (presumably from C Squadron, 2nd Fife and Forfar Yeomanry), which have been numbered (1). Other vehicles, presumably German given their location and direction of approach, are numbered (2). There is no obvious trace of the 88-mm flak guns in Cagny, although the orchard where they are sometimes claimed to have been deployed is numbered (3). It is worth mentioning that to have knocked out the tanks at (1), guns in this orchard would have had to fire through the broken hedgeline (no longer present) further west, numbered (4).
(Keele University Air Photo Archive)

the British made no attempt to occupy this critical feature. Instead, 2nd Fife and Forfar Yeomanry left its C Squadron to 'mask' Cagny, while the rest of the regiment pressed on towards the Bourguébus Ridge.

Manneville stud farm (*centre*), seen from Stand D4. 2nd Fife and Forfar Yeomanry's C Squadron was destroyed in the fields to the left of the track where the tractor is driving, probably by 88-mm flak guns deployed off the right hand side of the photo. *(SCT)*

The re-positioning of the *Luftwaffe* battery appears to have gone unnoticed by the crews of C Squadron's Shermans, sitting in the fields north-west of Cagny. Indeed, the first sign of the Germans' presence was when their guns opened fire shortly before 0930 hours.

Accounts of what happened next vary, as do the figures for British tanks destroyed. However, among the first tanks to be hit were those of C Squadron's commander, Major C. Nicholls (who was killed) and that of his second-in-command, Captain J. Miller. Several Shermans from B Squadron were knocked out around the same time, possibly by self-propelled guns from 4/200th Assault Gun Battalion, which was also in the Cagny area. Altogether, at least a dozen Shermans were 'brewed up', and C Squadron quickly ceased to exist as an organised or deployable unit.

Lt-Col Alec Scott, the Yeomanry's commander, reacted to C Squadron's demise by telling his attached infantry company (F/8th Rifle Brigade) to prepare an attack to capture Cagny. However, the order was countermanded by his superior, Brigadier Harvey, who was instructed by Maj-Gen Roberts to leave Cagny to follow-on

forces. Consequently, although part of 23rd Hussars moved up to replace C Squadron, the village remained in German hands.

During late morning the leading elements of 5th Guards Armoured Brigade approached Cagny from the north. Warned by Roberts that the village was strongly defended (in fact, despite von Luck's promise, few reinforcements ever arrived), and already heavily engaged near le Prieuré farm, their advance lacked momentum. Before midday 2nd (Armoured) Grenadier Guards pushed towards Cagny, but lost several tanks and came to a halt. At about 1530 hours the regiment tried again, sending half of No. 1 Squadron forward under the command of Captain J. Jones. Despite losing three tanks, this time the British established a foothold in the village, destroying two 88s and a Panzer IV. An attack was then organised by the motor infantry of the King's Company, 1st Grenadier Guards, who jumped off from near le Prieuré at 1730 hours. They encountered no opposition and, on entering Cagny, discovered that the Germans had abandoned their guns and withdrawn. After taking three prisoners, by 1830 hours the King's Company was disposed in defensive positions throughout the village. Later, other elements of the Guards Division arrived, and by nightfall the village was strongly held. Nevertheless, its defence had played a critical role for the Germans, both through the casualties and disruption caused by its defenders, and in buying vital time for *Major* von Luck to re-organise a line of resistance north of Frénouville.

Stand D5: Guards Armoured Division monument

DIRECTIONS: Return to your vehicle and turn right by the post office. Continue to the cemetery at the north-east corner of the village, which contains the graves of an RAF bomber crew killed on D-Day. Turn left onto the D225. After 500 metres, pull onto the verge, opposite the Guards Armoured Division monument.

THE SITE: Look at the monument and then at the surrounding countryside. Use the map to locate le Prieuré farm, Manneville Haras and Émiéville. Note the contrast between the undulating, close and marshy terrain nearby and the large open fields to the north, south and west. This was excellent defensive country, in which camouflaged anti-tank guns and small groups of infantry and armour could delay an attacker with relative ease. Large numbers of infantry were needed to overcome such defences;

1 1st (Armoured) Coldstream Guards, afternoon 18 July
2 2nd (Armoured) Grenadier Guards, afternoon 18 July
3 2nd (Armoured) Irish Guards, afternoon 18 July
4 2nd (Armoured Reconnaissance) Welsh Guards, 18 July
5 Elements 3rd British Infantry Division, 18 July
6 HQ 22nd Panzer Regiment, 1/503rd Heavy Tank Battalion, start of 18 July
7 22nd Panzer Regiment, start of 18 July
8 3/503rd Heavy Tank Battalion, start of 18 July
9 Elements 3/503rd Heavy Tank Battalion, late morning 18 July
10 1/503rd Heavy Tank Battalion, midday 18 July
11 Approximate German front line, end 18 July
Base map: IGN 1612OT
Touffréville
Sannerville
Démouville
To TROA
N175
To CAEN
To CAEN
N13
Émiéville
Cagny
Frénouville
D227
D225
D225a
To VIMONT
0
1
Kilometres

unfortunately, such troops were unavailable to the British forces that fought here on the opening day of Operation Goodwood.

THE ACTION: Little fighting took place in this area during the first hours of VIII Corps' attack. 11th Armoured Division was committed elsewhere, and the Guards Armoured Division was either stuck in traffic jams or tied down by the resistance around le Prieuré and Manneville (*see Stand D8*). For the Germans this respite was invaluable, and von Luck used it to re-deploy 21st Panzer Division's reconnaissance battalion from east of Troarn to positions north of Frénouville. Around midday these troops were joined by the 88-mm Pak 43s of 1039th Anti-Tank Battalion, plus a few Panzer IVs from I/22nd Tank Regiment. Together, they established a front protecting the road to Vimont, along which Guards Armoured Division was intending to advance towards its objectives.

The Guards Armoured Division memorial at Stand D5. *(SCT)*

By about 1600 hours German opposition around le Prieuré and Manneville was neutralised, and 2nd (Armoured) Irish Guards was ordered to advance to Vimont. No. 2 Squadron led, followed by the rest of the regiment. After crossing the Ruisseau de Cagny the British tanks continued south-east, but were held up by anti-tank fire on reaching the D225.

Pressing forward, part of No. 2 Squadron found several German tanks in the field opposite the Guards Division monument. There are so many versions of what happened next that the original war diary is quoted here in preference to the participants' own accounts:

'Lt J. Gorman's Troop on the left literally ran into 3 Panthers just over the crest. Lt Gorman rammed one – he was too

close and the Panthers too surprised for either to shoot – jumped out and led his crew back… L/Sjt Harbinson in the following tank was hit as he crossed the road Cagny – Émiéville and was badly wounded himself [he later died]. Of his crew L/Cpl Watson and Gdsm Davis were killed, and Gdsm Walsh and Gdsm Melville wounded. Of Lt Gorman's crew Gdsm Agnew and Gdsm Scholes were slightly wounded.

Back by the orchard Lt Gorman found L/Sjt Workman's Firefly. L/Sjt Workman had just been killed, though the tank was intact – so Lt Gorman pulled out the body and returned re-mounted to battle. Lt A.E. Dorman had by now reached the ridge and between them they shot up the two remaining Panthers which had withdrawn to the houses south of Émiéville.'

Source: 2nd (Armoured) Irish Guards War Diary, UK National Archives.

In fact, the tank rammed (and later destroyed) by Gorman was a King Tiger (a type the Guards had never seen before) from 1/503rd Heavy Tank Battalion, elements of which had arrived here following an abortive counter-attack further north (*see Stand D9*). The other panzers were probably Tiger Is or Panzer IVs; there were no Panthers nearby.

During the evening the Irish Guards continued probing towards

The wreck of Lt Gorman's Sherman *Ballyragget*, together with the King Tiger that he rammed and later destroyed. Gorman was awarded the Military Cross for this action, while L/Cpl James Baron, his driver, received the Military Medal.

Frénouville. However, although a few tanks reached the village, further progress was now impossible, and so the regiment leaguered near Cagny. At about 2200 hours the infantry of 3rd Irish Guards arrived, but no attempt was made to renew the advance next day. The Germans also brought up reinforcements from 12th SS Panzer Division. Although Frénouville was taken on 20 July, no further attacks were mounted in this direction, and Operation Goodwood effectively ended in the fields east of where you are now standing.

Stand D5, looking across the D225 towards Émiéville. The action in which Lieutenant Gorman knocked out the King Tiger took place in the far corner of the field on the right. *(SCT)*

Stand D6: Gouwy

DIRECTIONS: Continue along the D225 to Émiéville and turn left at the calvary. Drive about 1 km until you reach a church on your left. Park next to the war memorial, then cross the D225 and walk down the Rue Saint Rosaire for about 50 metres.

The access track to Stand D6 is straight ahead past the parked car in the middle of this photograph, which is taken looking east across the D225 at Gouwy. *(SCT)*

THE SITE: This is one of the most evocative locations on the Goodwood battlefield. Spend a few minutes looking around, noting the uneven ground amongst the trees and in the field beyond, evidence of one of the most concentrated bombardments ever unleashed in warfare.

THE ACTION: On 18 July the woods and orchards between Émiéville and Guillerville were occupied by most of I/22nd Panzer Regiment and part of its attached Tiger tank battalion. This position was relatively close to the front line, a fact which caused concern to *Major* von Luck, who would have preferred to have kept his armour where it was less likely to be observed or exposed to Allied fire.

As the air photo opposite shows, the German tank assembly was hit extremely hard by the RAF's bombers between 0545 and 0630 hours on 18 July. According to a detailed survey, no fewer than

his aerial photograph, taken on 18 July, shows Manneville stud farm and the deployment area of some of ne German armoured forces hit by the preliminary air bombardment. Stand D6 is numbered (1). Tank racks from the Tiger Is of 3/503rd Heavy Tank Battalion are visible at (2), while the tracks of the King Tigers f 1/503rd are prominent at top right (3), as they moved up to launch their counter-attack around midday, vhen this photograph was taken. The devastation on the right hand side of the photograph is in marked ontrast to the area at Manneville stud farm (left), which shows few signs of damage. *Keele University Air Photo Archive)*

145 bombs (500-lb or 1000-lb) fell in the 11-acre orchard which in 1944 occupied the site where you are now standing. Over 40,000 tons of earth was moved by the bombardment in the same area, and the Panzer IV company located here was annihilated. Four tanks were knocked out within 50 metres of the D225, and another 11 nearby; many transport vehicles were also destroyed.

This is one of the dozen or so tanks destroyed by the aerial bombing at Stand D6, in this case a Panzer IV of 22nd Panzer Regiment. *(IWM B8028)*

***Feldwebel* ((Sergeant) Korflür, a tank commander in 4/22nd Panzers, witnessed the bombers' arrival:**

'There was nothing left to do in the few seconds left except face the imminent death which had been reserved for us. Three comrades… snapped and fled: I never saw them again. After the first wave everybody was punch-drunk. We were going to put our camouflage back in order but were quickly spotted by the 'Jabos' [fighter-bombers] who were not going to let anyone out of this alive. I stayed under my tank through the second wave of bombing. At 0900 hours it was all over. Émiéville and our assembly area looked appalling: a few tanks had gone, the road had gone, and the quantity of craters edge to edge was such that it was virtually impossible to find the lane.'

Source: Jean-Claude Perigault, *21. Panzer-Division*, p. 520.

Despite the bombardment's effectiveness, the attackers were unable to exploit its effects. Determined opposition further north slowed British 3rd Infantry Division's advance, and the leading elements of 185th Brigade – responsible for clearing much of this area – only arrived near Guillerville in late afternoon. Consequently, the Germans had almost eight hours to repair damaged equipment. As a result, they sent over a dozen Panzer IVs into action as the day went on. Together with the surviving vehicles of 503rd Heavy Panzer Battalion, these made a valuable contribution to the defence of the south-east flank, albeit at a high price in men and tanks.

Stand D7: Manneville Haras (1)

DIRECTIONS: Rejoin your vehicle and continue along the D225, which meanders northwards, becoming the D227 in the process. Pass le Manoir farm and pull over. Look left through the hedge to a stone wall and woods 200 metres away. The area behind the wall was where the Tiger Is of 3/503rd Heavy Tank Battalion, commanded by the 22-year-old *Leutnant* Freiherr von Rosen, were located early on 18 July.

THE ACTION: 3/503rd's experience on 18 July was similar to that of I/22nd Panzers; von Rosen later described the air attack as the worst he ever experienced. One Tiger was overturned by the bombing and two others were destroyed. The rest were covered with earth and suffered varying amounts of damage. Nevertheless, because of the lack of infantry with which to clear the area, the British failed to prevent the Germans from digging their vehicles out, and by mid-morning *Leutnant* von Rosen had eight more or less serviceable tanks. Under instructions from his battalion commander, *Hauptmann* Fromme (whose headquarters in Émiéville survived the bombing), von Rosen moved his panzers along the wall surrounding the Manneville estate. Probably around 1030 hours, they reached the south-western side of Manneville farm, with the intention of counter-attacking into the left flank of the British armour that they could see heading south.

Stand D8: Manneville Haras (2)

DIRECTIONS: Continue along the D227 to a crossroads with a church on your right. Turn left and follow the road to the buildings of Manneville stud farm (this is private property, so please keep outside the perimeter wall). Look into the fields nearby, orientating yourself to earlier stands and the woods near le Prieuré farm.

THE SITE: With the obvious exception of the A13 road, this area has changed little since 1944. On 18 July it was the scene of persistent, heavy and very confused fighting. Several British units were involved at one time or another, including 23rd Hussars, most of 5th Guards Armoured Brigade and 2nd (Armoured Reconnaissance) Battalion, The Welsh Guards. Opposition came from various sources, including parts of 21st Panzer and 16th *Luftwaffe* Divisions. Most accounts also mention the presence early on of 5/200th Assault Gun Battalion, which was equipped with self-propelled multiple 81-mm mortars instead of the more typical 75-mm anti-tank guns and 105-mm howitzers.

The high stone wall around Manneville stud farm, behind which 3/503rd Heavy Tank Battalion was deployed on the morning of 18 July. The photograph is taken on the western side of the estate, looking north. *(SCT)*

THE ACTION: Soon after arriving near Manneville, 3/503rd's surviving Tigers moved forward to engage the British armour. However, as the leading panzers reached a position a few hundred metres south-west of Manneville two were knocked out, with their crews killed or wounded. Unusually, both tanks were disabled by rounds penetrating their frontal armour, something

Cromwell tanks of 2nd (Armoured Reconnaissance) Welsh Guards await the order to advance during Operation Goodwood. *(IWM B7740)*

the Germans thought their opponents' weapons could not do. (As suggested on p. 83, the *Luftwaffe* battery at Cagny may have been responsible.) Shocked by this sudden and unexpected loss, von Rosen ordered his remaining vehicles to withdraw, and they spent the rest of the day fighting off elements of Guards Armoured Division from positions near Émiéville. Both sides suffered losses and, although the British had the worst of it, von Rosen's company ended the day with only one serviceable tank.

Stand D9: Banneville-la-Campagne motorway bridge

DIRECTIONS: Return to the D227 crossroads, park, and walk north onto the bridge over the motorway. Look east to the scattered buildings around le Havre. Then face north-west, looking across a large field towards the hedgerows beyond.

THE ACTION: This was the scene of an unsuccessful counter-attack by 1/503rd's King Tigers at around midday on 18 July. Intended as a rescue mission for the German troops defending Démouville (*see Stand C4, pp. 147–9*), around half a dozen tanks participated. However, although they made their way without difficulty from le Havre to the D227 (which was lined in 1944 with a dense belt of trees), they came under heavy fire when they emerged into the field beyond. One King Tiger ran into a bomb crater, and two others were destroyed by direct hits (it is not known from what source; there were several British armoured and anti-tank units in this area). The others then withdrew south of Émiéville, where they joined the battle to prevent the Guards Armoured Division reaching Vimont (*see Stand D5*).

The view looking north-west from Stand D9, with the field in which 1/503rd's King Tigers came to grief in the foreground. Sannerville war cemetery lies behind the trees on the right hand side. *(SCT)*

ENDING THE TOUR: Continue north to Sannerville. Turn left onto the N175 towards Caen, and stop after 600 metres in the lay-by on the right, opposite the entrance to the Commonwealth War Graves Commission cemetery. There are 2,175 graves here, including many men who died during Operation Goodwood (most of the others are buried at Ranville war cemetery). After paying your respects, continue along the N175 back to Caen.

PART FOUR

ON YOUR RETURN

FURTHER RESEARCH

Most of the material for this book came either from personal accounts or from official sources, particularly documents in the National Archives of Great Britain, the National Archives of Canada, and the US National Archives and Records Administration (NARA), including translated German material. The authors are grateful for the assistance that they have received from these archives, and from other historians of the battle. The War Diaries (WO 171) and the official narratives (CAB 44) in the National Archives of Great Britain, were particularly valuable. There are many books dealing with various aspects of the battle for Caen, but just as episodes were controversial at the time so a considerable mythology has built up, and inaccurate statements have been repeated many times. The following books were useful, although in some cases the present authors may not share their conclusions.

The grave of Rex Whistler, the well known British painter, killed on 18 July near Manneville Haras and now buried in Sannerville cemetery. *(SCT)*

Ralph Bennett, *Ultra in the West: The Normandy Campaign 1944–45*; London, Hutchinson, 1979.

Eversley Belfield and Hubert Essame, *The Battle for Normandy*; London, Batsford, 1965.

Georges Bernages and Jean-Pierre Benamou, *Goodwood: Bombardement Géant Brise-Panzers*; Bayeux, Heimdal, 1994.

Terry Copp, *Fields of Fire: The Canadians in Normandy*; Toronto, University of Toronto Press, 2003.

Carlo d'Este, *Decision in Normandy*; London, Collins, 1983.

Above: The devastated city of Caen, seen on 10 July. *(IWM B6912)*

Page 185: Two soldiers of the Highland Light Infantry of Canada, Eddie Feltham (*left*) and John Cole, photographed after the bloody battle for Buron. *(NAC PA-131402)*

Christopher Dunphie, *The Pendulum of Battle: Operation Goodwood July 1944*; London, Leo Cooper, 2004.

L.F. Ellis, *Victory in the West*, Volume I: *The Battle of Normandy*; London, HMSO, 1962.

Roger A. Freeman, *The Mighty Eighth War Diary*; New York, Motorbooks, 1981.

Stephen Ashley Hart, *Montgomery and "Colossal Cracks": The 21st Army Group in Northwest Europe 1944–45*; London, Praeger, 2000.

F.H. Hinsley *et al.*, *British Intelligence in the Second World War*, Volume 3, Part 2; London, HMSO, 1988.

John Keegan, *Six Armies in Normandy*; London, Jonathan Cape, 1982.

Didier Lodieu, *45 Tiger en Normandie: la s. Pz. Abt. 503*; Louvers, Ysec, 2002.

Hans von Luck, *Panzer Commander*; New York, Dell, 1989.

Hubert Meyer, *The History of the 12. SS-Panzerdivision 'Hitlerjugend'*; Winnipeg, J.J. Federowicz, 1994.

Martin Middlebrook and Chris Everitt, *The Bomber Command War Diaries*; London, Midland Books, 1996.

Jean-Claude Perrigault, *21. Panzerdivision*; Bayeux, Heimdal, 2002.

Michael Reynolds, *Steel Inferno: I SS Panzer Corps in Normandy*; Staplehurst, Spellmount, 1977.

Pip Roberts, *From the Desert to the Baltic*; London, William Kimber, 1987.

Friedrich Ruge, *Rommel in Normandy*; London, Macdonald and Jane's, 1979.

Norman Scarfe, *Assault Division*; London, Collins, 1947.

John T. Sweet, *Mounting the Threat: The Battle of Bourguébus Ridge 18–23 July 1944*, Presidio Press, San Rafael, California, 1977.

Ken Tout, *The Bloody Battle for Tilly*; Thrupp, Sutton, 2000.

Russell F. Weighley, *Eisenhower's Lieutenants*; London, Sidgwick & Jackson, 1981.

David Westwood, *The German Army: Organisation and Personnel 1933–1945*; London, MLRS, 2004.

Niklas Zetterling, *Normandy 1944: German Military Effectiveness, Combat Power and Organizational Effectiveness*; Winnipeg, J.J. Federowicz, 2000.

Useful Addresses

UK National Archives, Public Record Office, Kew, Richmond, Surrey TW9 4DU; tel: 020 8876 3444; email: <enquiry@nationalarchives.gov.uk>; web: <www.nationalarchives.gov.uk>.

Imperial War Museum, Lambeth Road, London SE1 6HZ; tel: 020 7416 5320; email: <mail@iwm.org.uk>; web: <www.iwm.org.uk>.

Public Archives of Canada, 395 Wellington Street, Ottawa, Ontario K1A 0N3; tel: +01 613 9470 391.

US National Archives, The National Archives and Records Administration, 8601 Adelphi Road, College Park, MD 20740–6001; tel: +01 866 272 6272; web: <www.archives.gov>.

British Library, 96 Euston Road, London NW1 2DB; tel: 020 7412 7676; <email: reader-services-enquiries@bl.uk>.

University of Keele Air Photo Library, Keele University, Keele, Staffordshire ST5 5BG; tel/fax: 01782 583395; web: <evidenceincamera.co.uk>.

INDEX

Page numbers in *italics* denote an illustration.

Miles better for Normandy

Cruise to Cherbourg or Caen

Or race across to Cherbourg

If you're planning to visit the historic Normandy landing beaches, Brittany Ferries is the perfect choice.

Either sail in style from Poole or Portsmouth aboard one of our cruise ferries, or race across from Poole in just over 2 hours with our state-of-the-art fast ferry. No wonder Brittany Ferries is miles better.

PLYMOUTH
POOLE
PORTSMOUTH
CHERBOURG
CAEN
ROSCOFF
ST MALO

Reservations & Information

0870 908 9699

Brittany Ferries

www.brittanyferries.com